HANDBOOK OF
AIRCRAFT PERFORMANCE

HANDBOOK OF
AIRCRAFT PERFORMANCE

John H. H. Grover
FRAeS, MRIN, MBAC (Hon. Life)

Foreword by
Sir Peter Masefield

BSP PROFESSIONAL BOOKS
OXFORD LONDON EDINBURGH
BOSTON PALO ALTO MELBOURNE

Copyright © John H. H. Grover 1989

All rights reserved. No part of this
publication may be reproduced, stored
in a retrieval system, or transmitted,
in any form or by any means, electronic,
mechanical, photocopying, recording
or otherwise without the prior
permission of the copyright owner.

First published 1989

British Library
Cataloguing in Publication Data
Grover, John H.H.
  Handbook of aircraft performance
  1. aircraft, flying
  I. Title
  629,132'5

ISBN 0-632-02304-X

BSP Professional Books
A division of Blackwell Scientific
  Publications Ltd
Editorial Offices:
Osney Mead, Oxford OX2 0EL
  (Orders: Tel. 0865 240201)
8 John Street, London WC1N 2ES
23 Ainslie Place, Edinburgh EH3 6AJ
3 Cambridge Center, Suite 208, Cambridge
  MA 02142, USA
667 Lytton Avenue, Palo Alto, California
  94301, USA
107 Barry Street, Carlton, Victoria 3053,
  Australia

Photoset by Enset (Photosetting),
Midsomer Norton, Bath, Avon

Printed and bound in Great Britain by
Billings and Sons Ltd, Worcester

Contents

Foreword by Sir Peter Masefield	vii
Preface	ix
1 What Comprises a Runway?	1
2 Performance – General	10
3 Performance – Takeoff Requirements	20
4 Supplementary Takeoff Considerations	43
5 The Takeoff Flight Path	59
6 En Route	75
7 Descent and Landing	83
8 Additional Performance Considerations	99
9 Small Airliners	113
Appendix A Worked Example in Outline (BAe 146-100)	119
Appendix B Accident to DC–8-63 at Anchorage, 1970	122
Appendix C Accident to B737 at Washington DC, 1982	128
Comment on Appendices B and C	133
Glossary of Terms and Abbreviations	135
Index	139

Foreword
by Sir Peter Masefield

Practical experience applied to achievable performance against clear requirements – so as to get the best out of any man-made machine – are among the most basic factors for success in this age of technology; and nowhere more so than in the operation of modern aircraft.

The complexities are substantial – and increasing. The need for 'know-how' applied with understanding and judgement, is paramount. None of this can be gained quickly or easily.

All the more important, therefore, to garner and to absorb hard-won knowledge and experience based on a clear understanding of the requirements which, together, make for those essentials to success – safety, reliability and economy of operation.

For these reasons I especially welcome the gathering together in this book of an important compendium of the fruits of years of close involvement in British air transport on the part of John H.H. Grover. He brings to all that he has set down here a wide-ranging background of attainments and qualifications as a practical pilot, as a navigator, as a radio operator, as a route-planning and operations specialist and as an air traffic controller, in both civil air transport and in the Royal Air Force.

Years of study and of practice 'in the sharp end' are thus embodied in John Grover's important *Handbook of Aircraft Performance*. It cuts through some of the undergrowth which has grown up around the operational requirements for modern aircraft and it exposes to view how to look along the, sometimes turbulent, flight path ahead.

As we all know, there is often a gap between the word of official requirements and its application on to flight operations. In particular, the bald words of the official ICAO, BCAR, FAA and now EJAR requirements need explanation, interpretation and relating to everyday (and night) operations. John Grover provides that here.

As a modern example, the British Aerospace BAe 146 – the first new aircraft to be certificated under the European Joint Airworthiness Requirements (Part 25) – JAR 25 – well illustrates the application of the latest practice, through a comprehensive Flight Manual which takes into account not only JAR 25 but also those requirements covered by the United States Federal Aviation Regulations FAR 25 and by the British Civil Aircraft Requirements (BCAR Section D).

I warmly commend this excellent analysis and statement of 'What every good air transport should know'.

Finally, let me quote again those words of that earlier Churchill (The Reverend Charles), which I commended to my Flying Staff in the early days of BEA, so many years ago. They are as apposite today. He said:

> In full, fair, tide let information flow
> That trouble is half cured whose cause we know.

This book should cure a lot of troubles so often caused for want of clear information.

Sir Peter G. Masefield
'Rosehill'
Reigate

16th May 1988

Preface

In my opinion, all textbooks should have a preface that sets out clearly and unambiguously the aims and objectives of the book. It should also make clear the method of use of the book, and last but not least the author's motivation in writing the book. It is, of course, accepted that hopes of fame and fortune cannot be included in the last point – at least with regard to a textbook.

Throughout my aviation career I have not found a book that clearly explains either the current Performance Requirements (that is, the legally binding level of performance that is certificated by the appropriate authority), or the various dynamics, and their interaction, upon which these criteria are based. Thus my first aim is to explain to budding professional pilots the various requirements, as an aid to study, using simple non-official language. This has proved to be difficult, as when quoting from the requirements one must avoid changing the wording in case the legal sense is altered. Therefore, I have tried to interpret items that I have quoted verbatim, in order that some simplification may result. The material presented in this book only refers to the more modern 'Performance Group A' or Transport category aircraft and excludes the more venerable types and also helicopters.

The performance examinations set by the various authorities essentially seek to ensure that the candidate can use a Flight Manual correctly. I believe that it is in a pilot's best interests if he (or she) knows at least *something* about what lies behind the Flight Manual scheduled performance. Pilots like to know what is behind the various actions and decisions that they are required to take. But they do not want to be deluged with a plethora of scientific jargon and formulae. This goes for students too. I have therefore tried to present the requirements – be they British Civil Airworthiness Requirements, Joint Airworthiness Requirements, or the US Federal Aviation Regulations (BCAR Section D, JAR 25, and FAR 25) – in a readable form. When using the word 'airworthiness' I am, of course, referring to performance only, and not to structures. There are also certain *operating* regulations that have to be observed, such as FAR 121, the UK Air Navigation Order and Regulations.

The first aim, therefore, is to present a study guide for students and a refresher for qualified pilots, together with the reasons for details that are 'hidden' in the material that they are required to learn and to know. For example, how many experienced pilots really know what is involved in the Decision Speed, V_1?

Now to the second element. To make the fullest use of this book I have deliberately introduced 'Comment' paragraphs, where I have discussed certain points and, in my opinion, shortcomings in the various requirements. These are few, but I feel that it should be clearly understood that they are there. That there are some shortcomings is scarcely surprising in view of the immensity of the task involved in scheduling the performance of today's modern and complex aircraft. My comments must not be construed in any way as impugning the regulatory authorities. I believe that my experience as an airline technical pilot, allied to my long specialisation in aircraft performance matters, has given me valuable insight into performance and performance-related matters that will not normally be found in the 'rule book'. As a result, I want to make the reader *think* and not take the regulatory requirements for granted. I believe that a number of pilots would still be alive today, had they not slavishly followed the requirements without question. But I want this to be a quest for knowledge and an understanding of the reasons why certain things are done – and the limitations that are involved. I do *not* want student readers to start questioning the requirements and discussing any shortfalls in the course of their taking the official examinations for their licences. It should not be forgotten that the examiners, in most cases, are part of the body that lays down, and enforces, the requirements. If you have any doubts, or wish to query any requirements, do this either with your instructors, or with your colleagues once you have your licence! My 'Comment' paragraphs are designed to promote thought and discussion; if you think that, occasionally, the law is an ass, then think why, and discuss this with your colleagues. Then, and only then, see if you can induce the law to mend its ways. It has been done – often – by thinking pilots.

The 'Comment' paragraphs will be clearly indicated as such – i.e. **Comment**. They represent the author's personal opinions although most have the support of professional pilots worldwide. I have, I hope, substantiated the reasoning behind these 'Comment' sections by reference to either factual situations – e.g. official accident reports – or by illustrated circumstances in which it can be shown that a situation could arise, however improbable, that is not covered by the scheduled performance. In such cases I have tried to offer a reasoned remedy to the shortfall. Other than in these 'Comment' paragraphs, or unless clearly indicated, all material in this book is based on the various requirements and it has been my hope that by knowing both the requirements *and* their background an increased level of understanding will result and that with this will come an increased awareness and concomitant safety level.

Now, my motivation in writing this book. First, I feel that all too often important study material is forgotten once the student has gained his (or her) licence. Yet the basis of an aircraft's performance is vital information and is called upon for every flight. I have known of one airline, for example, where the ground and flight management considered that certified performance considerations were subject to the eleventh Commandment – 'Thou shalt not be found out'. Throughout this airline's existence an accident was waiting to happen. Mercifully, before disaster struck the airline went out of business!

In the interests of safety I want to share my experience with others. I have worked with many regulatory authorities, and have discussed performance matters in depth with my peers and colleagues. I have flown on performance related matters in the UK, Europe and the USA, and as a result have learned much. A truly good pilot never stops learning – ever. Those who feel that they have no more to learn are, in fact, well on the way to the obituary columns, and, if flying an airliner, are likely to be taking others with them. Remember the old dictum – 'There are old pilots, and there are bold pilots. But there are *very* few old *and* bold pilots'. So keep thinking, questioning, and learning. Perhaps then, in time, you will become a good pilot.

Although this is a manual of aircraft performance I should, perhaps, emphasise that it deals only with Certificated Performance matters. Other performance aspects will be dealt with in a companion volume, *Airline Route Planning*, currently in the course of preparation.

Finally, I would like to thank those who have given me both help and encouragement in the writing of this book. I would like to thank British Aerospace Hatfield (Mr Malcolm Galbraith) and Filton (Mr David Rowe) for providing me with a Flight Manual to work my examples from, and copies of other regulatory documents. I am also grateful for the British Aerospace photographs provided by Mr Hugh Field, of BAe, Hatfield and to Fokker BV for Plate 5. And last, but far from least, I am indebted to my colleague Sir Peter Masefield (President of the Association of British Aviation Consultants) for writing a foreword to this book so willingly, and advising me as regards certain improvements to the text!

June 1988

1: What Comprises a Runway?

One is inclined, initially anyway, to think of a 'runway' as being simply a length of concrete or tarmac upon which aircraft takeoff and land. On closer inspection this is found to be far from being the case. A runway can consist of up to three separately defined elements lengthwise – i.e. the actual basic runway itself, plus possibly a further extension that is more 'lightly engineered' known as Stopway, plus a further possible extension lengthwise that is not engineered, but is clear of any non-frangible obstacles, and is known as Clearway. Thus a runway may consist of up to three lateral dimensions. It may also have a vertical variation defined, this being the Slope, and a datum elevation above (or in some cases below) sea level. To the whole, although not performance-related, (directly) may be added a lighting installation and radio navigational aids.

In tackling any exposition on aircraft performance the initial problem is where to begin. The logical answer is, of course, to begin at the beginning. But this in itself raises a new question – where is the beginning? Or, to be more specific, do the aircraft performance requirements in being, dictate the runway characteristics or vice versa? Clearly the aircraft performance requirements not only vary from type to type but also from flight to flight. As an 'adjustable' runway is, of course, out of the question, it must follow that all airport runways should be suitable for all aircraft types that are likely to use them. Thus, in broad terms, most runways are built to a 'standard' pattern, with aircraft performance characteristics being dictated by these runways.

With supersonic aircraft travel now firmly established, it should be noted that the aircraft involved were designed to use existing runways serving the routes for which these aircraft were designed. With new 'orbital' types for the future now being discussed it seems logical to assume that these proposed aircraft will not be favoured operationally, at least, if they require dedicated long and strong runways significantly in excess of those already in existence. So one is forced to recognise that the point from which to commence any work on aircraft performance is an explanation of what, exactly, comprises a runway and its characteristics. But it is still necessary, at this point, to set down very broadly, what is involved in a commercial aircraft's runway performance. Please note that this book does not attempt to deal with light, or recreational aircraft, helicopters, or the older 'unclassified' transport category types.

All modern 'transport category' (i.e. large airliners, exceeding 5700 kg maximum all-up weight) have runway performance scheduled in a document called the Flight Manual, and this Manual forms part of the aircraft's Certificate of Airworthiness. An engine failure is assumed to occur during the takeoff, while the landing is often assumed to take place with one engine inoperative. The Landing Distance requirement may be scheduled either with all-engines operating *or* with an engine-out. If all-engines are assumed then reverse thrust may not be taken into account, to meet the requirement that allowance must be made for failure of means of retardation. It is usual, therefore, to schedule the shorter distance measured, according to the aircraft's characteristics. As regards the takeoff, a Decision Point is calculated before each departure, this Decision Point being identified by the attainment of a given speed, known as the Decision Speed, or in abbreviated form, V_1. Should an engine fail at, or before, V_1 the takeoff must, by regulation, be abandoned (or aborted, or rejected, to use other expressions currently in use). Should the engine failure occur at a speed above V_1 the takeoff must be continued. The runway must be long enough to permit the safe execution of either of these courses, in safety.

A runway will normally have its characteristics published in the appropriate State's Aeronautical Information Publication (AIP), and also in a commercially-produced Flight Guide (e.g. Aerad or Jeppesen). The first point to consider is that a runway may consist of a number of separately defined distances, or in many cases just one. Let us first of all see what is required of a runway, in terms of distance(s) by the various performance requirements.

The Takeoff Surface, or Runway

First of all, there must be sufficient prepared surface for the aircraft to accelerate to its all-engines lift-off speed (V_{LOF}) and then climb away. (A third of the distance from lift-off to the screen is added.) This distance is referred to as the Takeoff Run. The next requirement is that the aircraft must have sufficient distance to accelerate to the Decision Speed V_1 previously referred to, and then experience an engine failure, and then continue to accelerate using its remaining engine(s) to its lift-off speed, at which it becomes airborne. The runway distance available for this latter purpose is known as the TakeOff Run Available (TORA) and this is the first published distance. It is rarely significant, in isolation, from the performance point of view.

Secondly, there must be sufficient distance for the aircraft, having

WHAT COMPRISES A RUNWAY?   3

engine failure at, or after, V_1 to accelerate using its remaining engine(s) so as to become airborne and then to continue to accelerate until it reaches an imaginary 35 ft screen, crossing this at its takeoff Safety Speed (V_2). The runway distance available for this procedure is known as TakeOff Distance Available (TODA). This distance is, as in the case of TORA, duly promulgated in the publications mentioned above.

Thirdly, there must be sufficient distance for an aircraft to experience an engine failure at, or before V_1. In this case the distance available must be sufficient to reach V_1 and then to abort (refuse, reject, abandon, etc.) the takeoff and come to a halt within the runway distance available for this situation. This significant total distance is known as the Emergency Distance Available (EMDA) or the Accelerate Stop Distance Available (ASDA). (See Fig. 1.1.)

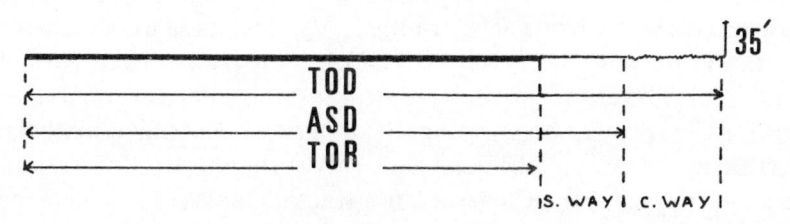

Fig. 1.1 The elements that make up a 'runway' for the takeoff calculation

Finally there is the Landing Distance Available (LDA). This is a more or less simple statement of fact. However, the requirement to clear all obstacles on the Approach, at a speed not less than $1.3 \times$ stalling speed ($1.3 \times V_S$) usually based on a 3° glide slope, may mean that the landing threshold has to be displaced away from the runway-beginning until the glide slope clears all obstacles on the Approach that penetrate the plane of the glide slope. Both LDA and EMDA/ASDA are promulgated, as with TORA and TODA. (Fig. 1.2 shows the UK 30 ft Screen Height. FAR 25 and JAR 25 prescribe 50 ft, but JARs allow a choice between the two.)

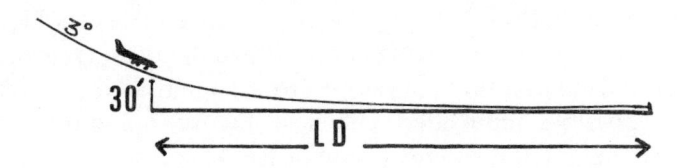

Fig. 1.2 The derivation of landing distance required; the 3° glide slope is normal, but may be greater for certain operations

It now falls to show how the runway, as somewhat loosely described up to now, is made up from anything from one to three elements. Firstly there is the runway proper; that is to say the concrete, tarmac, or concrete and tarmac strip that will be familiar to most readers. As mentioned earlier, this engineered strip can form the total operational runway. In other words, TORA = TODA = EMDA(ASDA), for takeoff purposes. However, in addition to this runway proper there may also be available a form of extension at the end of the takeoff direction. This extension is not engineered to anything like the same standard as the TORA runway, and may well consist merely of hard ground free of obstacles. Its sole purpose is to allow an aircraft that has aborted its takeoff from a high value of V_1 to overrun the prepared runway and come to a halt within the extension without sustaining other than slight or superficial damage. This extension is referred to as *Stopway*. The TORA+Stopway = EMDA/ASDA. A third element, comprising obstacle-free terrain over which an aircraft may fly while accelerating to V_2, is referred to as *Clearway*. TORA+Stopway+Clearway = TODA. Clearway need not be solid; it may be entirely over water, for instance, or over rough grass. But for Clearway to be promulgated it *must* be controlled by the airport, to avoid mobile obstacles suddenly springing up. For example, no ships may cross the Clearway, nor tractors, unless specifically permitted to do this by the airport for each occasion. Total Clearway may not exceed ½ TORA. A 'Balanced Field' exists where TODA = ASDA. Figure 1.1 shows how the total takeoff operational runway plane surface is made up.

The Landing Distance Available may not exceed the TORA. It assumes a 30 ft imaginary screen at the beginning of the runway (50 ft for FAR 25 and JAR 25), over which passes a 3° glide slope. The end of the LDA is normally coincident with the end of the TORA; and Stopway may *not* form part of the LDA. At times circumstances may arise, or exist, that cause the LDA to be less than the TORA. A typical example may be seen in the case where a motorway, or road, crosses the extended centreline of the LDA in the direction towards the Approach. If this road passes too close to the runway high-sided vehicles may penetrate the 3° glide slope on occasion. The remedy is for the airport authority to declare a Displaced Threshold, which involves the screen height being moved down the runway, away from the threshold, so that the glide slope crosses the road high enough to clear all possible high-sided vehicles. Figure 1.2 illustrates the philosophy behind the promulgation of LDA.

Runway Slope

Now we turn to a runway characteristic that causes a certain amount of head-scratching – and understandably so! This is the Slope (%) of the runway, and is expressed as being Uphill or Downhill. A runway's Slope is not normally promulgated, as such. Instead the elevations above Mean Sea Level are given for either threshold, and the difference, as an item of rise or fall, is applied to the total EMDA/ASDA, and to the TODA so as to establish the percentage the vertical value forms of the horizontal value. At this point it must be mentioned that, in the Western world, it is normal to express vertical distances in feet, and horizontal ones in metres. However, for illustration purposes we will consider a typical case in feet throughout.

Consider a runway (TODA = EMDA/ASDA = TORA) of 10 000 feet length. The elevation of the takeoff end is given as being 200 ft above mean sea level (amsl), and that of the upwind end 280 ft amsl (above mean sea level). We thus have a height difference of 80 ft between the two ends of the runway, and the fact that the upwind end is the higher means that there is an Uphill Slope for the takeoff in question. 80 ft is 0.8% of 10 000 ft and so we have a 0.8% Uphill Slope to be considered for all takeoff calculations using this runway; this is the usual practice in such circumstances, and is normally permitted by the regulatory authorities.

Comment

Is the figure calculated thus necessarily valid in all cases where there is a Slope? That is to say, where the difference in elevations, applied to length of runway, produces this figure mathematically, e.g. when the runway length is as given above and the elevation difference is 80 ft. Or, where the elevation difference is, say, 40 ft and the runway length is 5000 ft, and so on. The answer must be that the Slope calculation based on this formula can only be truly valid in those cases where the elevation change is constant along the runway.

If we continue with the example being used as an academic illustration, what is the true Slope, for calculation purposes, when the runway elevation rises, for instance, at the midway point to, say, 350 ft? Here we have a 0.8% overall Uphill Slope, *but* at the 5000 ft point the actual elevation is not 40 ft but no less than 150 ft. The slope up to the midway point is, in fact, no less than 3.0% Up, while for the remainder of the runway it is 1.4% Down (350 ft−280 ft = 70 ft (100/5000×70 = 1.4%). Bearing in mind that the first half of the runway is now 3% Up, this must increase the acceleration adversely, up to the midway point, while beyond that a Downhill slope is obtained of 1.4%. This, in turn, must adversely affect the deceleration in any aborted takeoff. So, in the case under consideration we have, taking the EMD(ASD) alone as an example, a totally different picture than that presented by the constant 0.8% gradient assumed. In fact, in the aborted takeoff case the acceleration sector *required* will be greater, and so will the deceleration sector, than that portrayed. (Assuming that the Decision Point/ V_1 is around the mid-point along the runway). So the EMD(ASD) *required* will be greater on this runway than on a runway having the same length and similar elevations but having a constant gradient of 0.8% Uphill.

As regards the effect on the TOD, the illustrated case with its mid-point 'humped' runway, will also produce a different picture. Here we have a labouring, uphill, acceleration element to the Decision Point (V_1) for most, if not all, of the way. (This V_1 point must be displaced downwind as a result of the Slope profile under discussion.) If, using the 0.8% Uphill Slope for the pre-takeoff calculation, it is found that most – if not all – of the runway (10 000 ft) is required then there will be less distance to accelerate with an engine-out to V_2 at the 35 ft screen, (or in some earlier cases 50 ft). But, against this must be borne in mind the fact that most, if not all, of this distance is *Downhill,* which will both improve the acceleration *and* reduce the engine-out acceleration distance required. Also, of course, the ground is dropping away from the flight path, thus moving the screen downwards, somewhat improving the screen clearance vertical distance.

This illustration is based on a fictitious runway with a midway 'humped' profile. Now consider the case using the same figures as those used for the illustration but where the peak elevation, or 'hump', is moved towards the start of the takeoff end of the runway, or towards the lift-off end. In the first case the acceleration sector will be even more adversely affected initially, followed by an improvement due to the subsequent Downhill gradient. But the 'budgeted-for' deceleration sector will also be Downhill, instead of 0.8% Uphill, thus increasing the distance required for deceleration, with the total EMD(ASD) required also being increased. With the high-point being moved to the opposite—i.e. lift-off—end we have a substantially increased Uphill Slope for the acceleration sector, followed by a sharp Downhill Slope for the remainder. Once again, the EMD(ASD) *required* will exceed that calculated when using a linear 0.8% Uphill Slope as is normally the practice.

There are almost infinite permutations that can make the Slope value difficult, if not impossible, to calculate to a nicety, and thus the geographical position of the Decision Point can vary due to the Slope profile. Consider the opposite situation to that being discussed, where the runway is 'dished' instead of being 'humped'. In this new case we accelerate Downhill – a good thing, and decelerate Uphill – another good thing, in the EMD(ASD) case. But in the continued takeoff engine-out case the ground is rising, impairing the engine-out acceleration after V_1 (if still on the runway) and raising the screen towards the airborne flight path, which is of no help!

How can these (fortunately rare and often hypothetical) situations be resolved? And what of the aircraft type that may only need half of the runway? For example, a 10 000 ft runway can be limiting to, say a Boeing 747, while a Fokker F27 could probably find 5000 ft perfectly adequate. The

B747 is almost certainly going to need all the 10 000 ft, and perhaps more if heavily loaded, and will thus be affected by the Slope *profile*, as discussed. The F27, on the other hand, will probably only need the first 5000 ft or so and will therefore not be affected by the slope of the remaining part of the runway, unless in the rare or unlikely case of this slope being so steep as to penetrate the airborne flight path.

Performance considerations are dealt with elsewhere, and this chapter is concerned only with the Runway. However, in this context it is worth mentioning that most major airports publish a plan of their runway(s) profile(s) through the medium of the national AIP, this document having already been referred to earlier. This plan is known as the International Civil Aviation Organisation (ICAO) Type 'A' Chart, and clearly shows, in most cases, the divergence of the actual runway profile from a linear constant gradient resulting from the difference between the elevations of the ends of the runway being portrayed. However, using the Type 'A' Chart can enable only the length of the runway required to be taken into account as regards the Slope. Thus, for the F27 approximately the first 5000 ft only would need to be taken into account as regards the Slope calculation, and should there be significant variations in elevation in this element – i.e. should this distance be either 'humped' or 'dished' – the F27 Flight Manual contains information to enable the takeoff calculation to divide the EMD(ASD) into two separate parts as regards the distance, so that the appropriate Slope value can be used for each part, as appropriate. At least the average Slope up to the Decision Point (V_1) and the average slope for the deceleration element following an aborted takeoff from V_1 can be used to provide a more accurate Slope value for each sector, the sum of the two independently calculated distances being the EMD(ASD) required, and to a higher degree of accuracy.

Landing Runway – Some Complications
So much for the takeoff case, when considering a runway. The Landing case is far simpler, as there is only one element. The Landing Distance Available (LDA) is normally based on a 3° Approach Slope, as described earlier in this chapter. Sometimes though, the terrain on, or near to, the Approach path will dictate a steeper Approach Slope – e.g. Innsbruck, Austria. Normally the 3° Approach and Landing Slope will cross the landing runway threshold so as to clear an imaginary 30 ft screen at the threshold. However, in certain cases – e.g. a major road that crosses the centre line of the Approach close to the runway, this road being outside the control of the airport – obstacles may sometimes penetrate the Approach slope. In the case of a road these obstacles may be moving, such as high-sided vehicles (one remedy, by the way, that will avoid such penetration is for the airport to be able to control traffic on the road by means of traffic lights).

Here the Landing threshold must be displaced away from the threshold so that the Approach Slope crosses the road high enough to allow adequate clearance beneath for the largest, tallest, vehicles to pass below the 3° Approach slope. The same applies to those cases where obstacles are fixed, such as a building.

Runway Slope must be taken into account, particularly when the runway may be limiting. Here the actual runway profile may exert some effect, and once again the Type 'A' Chart can give more accurate slope data than that obtained by the change in the two threshold elevations. There is also a substantial increment added to an aircraft's measured landing performance to allow for handling variations and small errors, such as deviation from the Approach Slope, so that the runway slope is not quite so significant when considering the Landing case due to the fact that the aircraft is decelerating intentionally, plus the fact that the Landing Distance Required (either Destination or Alternate) contains a very hefty factor.

Surface Wind and Elevation

Two other items of runway, or airport data need to be considered. As regards the runway the Wind Component – i.e. the value of the actual wind direction and speed, corrected for the runway's alignment – needs to be known for the takeoff calculation. Naturally, as this will be changing all the time it cannot be promulgated. A Headwind down the runway shortens the required distances TOR/TOD/EMD(ASD), LD, while a Tailwind increases them.

The second item of data concerns the airport itself. It is necessary to know its height above sea level for planning V_2 Climb-calculation purposes. This altitude is also promulgated, as in the case of runway data. Incidentally, not all airports are at, or above, sea level; Amsterdam (Schiphol) is 13 ft below, for example.

Any *promulgated* altitude, or elevation, will be in height Above Mean Sea Level (amsl). This is a purely geographical value, derived by surveyors and is exactly what it says. However, when we come to deal with the actual performance of an aircraft we shall need to take into account either, or both, Pressure Altitude and Density Altitude. The former is an international standard and is the altitude with the altimeter (or a barometer) set to the international barometric element of the International Standard Atmosphere, namely 1013.2 mb or 29.92 Hg (inches of mercury). International Standard Atmosphere (ISA) is based on a sea-level temperature of 15°C at this pressure; the specified density is 0.002378 slugs per cubic ft (ft^3). Density Altitude is a function of temperature and Pressure Altitude–e.g. if the Pressure Altitude is 3000 ft and the True Air Temperature is +25°C the Density

Altitude will be 5000 ft. It is not necessary to learn the conversion formula as all pilot's navigation computers have a conversion scale and this is the normal method of calculation of such values. Most Flight Manual takeoff and landing charts are based on Pressure Altitude and are clearly labelled so.

2: Performance – General

Since the first aeroplane flew it was subject to the laws governing flight performance, and all other aircraft subsequently have been similarly affected. For many years little was done to quantify these laws, although they did find their way into the science and art of aerodynamics. Initially it was found that aircraft X needed y ft in which to takeoff and land, while simple observations similarly established that this aircraft took z minutes to climb to different indicated altitudes, the time naturally depending on the altitude. Variations in distances or times were probably known to be a function of the ambient temperature and possibly even of Density Altitude.

The aircraft designed and built between the two World Wars showed a distinct trend towards the inclusion of aerodynamic knowledge having been incorporated in their design – even wind tunnels were in use by then. But very little data was available, as regards performance matters, to their pilots. At the best a slim volume, entitled *Pilots Notes* and covering a specific type of aircraft, was made available. Although mainly an advisory volume on the handling characteristics of the type of aircraft covered, it did provide an element of performance data. But such data was rudimentary and although very meagre it was a step in the right direction and better than nothing.

After the end of World War II nearly all civil airliners were, for the first few years at least, either conversions of military transport aircraft, these mainly requiring furnishing or 'cosmetic' modifications, or else were direct adaptations of the larger bombers. But there were cases where airliners did start their lives as such, before the war, becoming transports or outright combat aircraft during the war, and then, in *most* cases, reverting back to their original role. Perhaps the classic example, and one that at the time of writing is still in airline service worldwide, is the Douglas DC–3. The Dutch airline KLM operated DC–3s in Europe in the late 1930s, for example. This excellent aircraft became the prolific C–47 Dakota during the war, and then returned to airline service as either the DC–3 or Dakota, in large numbers.

The German Focke-Wulf company produced a large, four-engined, airliner at about the same time. This became the maritime reconnaissance bomber known as the Kondor, having in its original form, been blessed with the unwarlike name Kurier. In the UK, Shorts built the 'Empire' flying boat, which became the Sunderland, which in turn became the peacetime Hythe, Sandringham, and Solent. The US B-29 bomber became the Stratocruiser, while the wartime Avro York continued into peacetime, like the DC-3, as an airliner.

In the early post-war years civil airliners, whether ex-military transports or new designs, were provided with far more detailed performance data, this being based on measured flight performance. In the early post-war years great excitement was aroused by the requirement for performance not only to be scheduled but also for the inclusion of engine-out Climb ability accountable to altitude and to temperature. In the event of an engine failure on takeoff the aircraft had to be able to maintain a positive gradient of climb, and if necessary the weight proposed for takeoff had to be reduced until the requirement was reached. A performance document (albeit, somewhat rudimentary in its contents) known as the Performance Schedule, was issued and formed part of the Certificate of Airworthiness. However, the point at which the engine failure occurred was somewhat vague. Nevertheless, flight performance was being documented, by regulation.

It was not long before a far more comprehensive scheduling of civil airliner's performance, among other things, became more detailed, while the performance requirements became more stringent. In fact, the basis for these requirements remains virtually valid for the present day, although they have become even more elaborate, and improved. The Performance Schedule gave way for new designs, to an imposing document called the 'Flight Manual'.

Decision Point or Speed
Just as Weight, Altitude and Temperature (WAT) performance had been introduced a few years earlier, so was a new concept introduced with the Flight Manual. This was the assumption that, for every takeoff an engine would fail during the takeoff, and that an engine failure would also occur during the flight (the latter rule was already in force). Thus, during the takeoff, should an engine fail, it was, and is, a legal requirement that it must *either* be able to abandon (or abort, or reject) the takeoff safely *or* continue the takeoff with an engine inoperative. This was a significant improvement on the previous situation under which, in the event of engine failure, a devout but perforce short prayer was the best aid.

Naturally, where the engine failed during takeoff was a very major consideration. It was necessary for the pilot to know when he could still abort his takeoff safely, and when it was unsafe to do so but safe to continue. In the aircraft type's certification programme, flight tests were conducted so as to derive the all-engines acceleration, and acceleration with an engine-out. This flight testing had to be conducted in varying conditions of weight, altitude, and temperature, and in sufficient numbers of flights to enable a standard level of performance to be established over a wide range of conditions.

In order that the requirements could be met, it became necessary to establish a Decision Point. Should an engine fail before, or at this point, it had to be possible to abandon the takeoff and then bring the aircraft to a halt without causing anything more than superficial damage to the aircraft. Should the engine fail at, or after the Decision Point, the aircraft was required to be able to accelerate with an engine-out and then to become airborne and to clear an imaginary 50 ft screen. This screen height was later reduced to 35 ft and this remains the case today, as do the foregoing requirements. The Decision Point, for any particular aircraft, varies from takeoff to takeoff. It therefore begs the question – how is it identified? The answer is that each and every Decision Point calculated for the conditions actually obtaining is linked to Indicated Airspeed (IAS). Therefore, the Decision Point, although expressed in terms of distance is actually established by the attainment of a prescribed value of IAS. (In fact, the expression 'Decision Point' is only to be found, normally, in BCARs, Section D, now superseded by JAR 25.)

The Flight Manual contains data that enables the pilot to calculate a number of takeoff parameters, and these relate to the runway in use, as has been defined in Chapter 1. In the first case, the pilot must be able to see that the Takeoff Run Available (TORA) is sufficient. Secondly he, or she, must also check that the all-engines takeoff distance available is sufficient. Then the required EMD (ASD) must be checked against the EMDA (ASDA), and the engine-out Takeoff Distance Required and that actually available – i.e. TOD required and TODA. But here comes the rub – the ASD (EMD) required, and the TOD required, both depend upon the location of the Decision Point, or speed V_1. And TOD required varies with V_1 and the required screen speed (a function of weight), V_2. The higher the ratio between $V_1:V_2$ (now $V_1:V_R$, this latter being Rotation Speed, which is linked to V_2) the higher the distance required to V_1, or the higher the weight that the TODA will allow for takeoff. Conversely, the ASD (EMD) required to reach V_1 and then allow for the takeoff to be abandoned, varies with V_1, through the ratio $V_1:V_R$. Thus, the

PERFORMANCE – GENERAL   13

higher ratio–and hence V_1–the greater is the distance required to meet the EMD required.

Let us elaborate a little on this interaction. Climb gradient depends on speed – the higher the speed at liftoff the better the climb-out gradient, and thus the V_1 point may be brought closer to the 35 ft screen. But, for the same weight as in the TOD case, the higher the speed V_1 the greater is the need for distance to come to a stop, in the case of engine failure at V_1. Thus we have two conflicting interests and a compromise between the two must be established.

As TOD and EMD interact against each other when seeking to establish the V_1 value necessary for the calculation of either the Maximum Takeoff Weight or TOD and EMD required, these two parameters were accurately measured during the flight test programme, and after the inclusion of certain safety factors (these will be gone into in more detail later), plus Standard Deviations to allow for handling differences etc, plus certain operating inaccuracies such as Slope (see Chapter 1), graphical information for each parameter was provided in the Flight Manual.

In these early Flight Manual charts cognisance had to be taken of, in each case, Temperature, Elevation, Weight, $V_1:V_2$, Slope, and Wind Component. But, it will be said by many, at this point we do not know the ratio $V_1:V_2$. Very true, but we can now find out, even

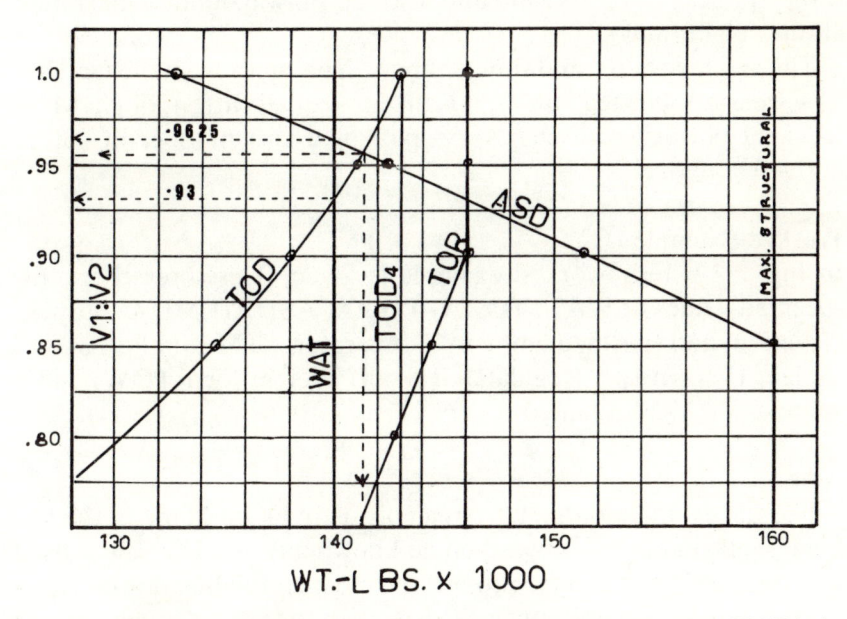

Fig. 2.1 The basis of the Regulated Takeoff Weight calculation. Here WAT is the limiting factor

though this involves much accurate extraction of data from the charts, and by plotting this on graph paper. The process is as follows, assuming that we are, in this case, trying to establish the Maximum all-up weight (Maximum auw), and $V_1:V_2$ from a runway whose distances are known. (Fig. 2.1.)

Firstly, take either the EMD(ASD) or TOD engine-out chart. Taking the actual, or expected temperature, proceed to the airfield altitude and from there find the curve applicable to weight variations. Pencil in thinly this applicable curve in the 'family' of printed weight curves on the chart. Now, assuming that we are using the EMD(ASD) chart, enter with the EMD available, correct for wind and Slope, as appropriate, and then move to the $V_1:V_2$ ratio grid. Quite arbitrarily, select at least three separate, and spaced ratios – e.g. 1.0, 0.95, 0.90 and 0.85. From each ratio selected now move, in turn, to the pencilled weight curve. You will find that, for these ratios, four different weight values will result. Take a sheet of graph paper and simply plot a curve for $V_1:V_2$ versus weight. (It is preferable to plot the ratio vertically, and the weight horizontally.) As the ratio is increased so will the weight reduce.

Now repeat the procedure, but using the TOD engine-out chart, and again plot the results. Draw a curve, as before, on the same sheet of graph paper. This time the weight will increase with a ratio increase, and the two curves will intersect. The point of intersection is the applicable $V_1:V_2$ ratio and also the runway-limited maximum all-up weight (auw).

This is a laborious, and slow business. Yet, apart from the fact that now we use V_R instead of V_2, it is the basis of all current Flight Manual field performance charts – a plot of a vast number of values derived as above.

Worked Example
In Fig. 2.1 a fully worked example is given. This shows how, for specified values of WAT, TORA, TODA, ASDA(EMDA), airfield elevation, and specified ambient Temperature, a Maximum Takeoff Weight (known as a Regulated Takeoff Weight, or RTOW) and a value of $V_1:V_2$ is obtained.

Note
While the example is taken from an obsolete Flight Manual, the airfield is imaginary and is based on no known airport. The values used have been selected so as to provide the most useful illustration. However, *if* this airport and runway exists, then the results calculated are appropriate.

In Fig. 2.1 a high altitude has been chosen for the airport so that WAT is a significant factor. It will be seen that the TORA, TODA, and EMDA produce two intersections when plotted against each other. As is normally the case, the interaction between TODA and EMDA produces the *apparent* RTOW (141 350 lb), reading vertically downward from the intersection of their plots, and also the *apparent* value of $V_1:V_2$ (0.955), reading horizontally to the left. (Incidentally, when TORA becomes the significant value this is normally due to large values of Clearway and of Stopway. During the continued takeoff case both of these may only be flown over, the aircraft becoming airborne within the distance afforded by TORA.) But note the position of the WAT limit vertical line. This lies to the left of the TODA and EMDA intersection, and is therefore more limiting (140 000 lb). It also invalidates the $V_1:V_2$ ratio produced by these two distances. Instead it produces *two* $V_1:V_2$ intersections (0.93 and 0.9625), and therefore two values of V_1 (113.5 kt to 118 kt). But, by Regulation, a specified V_1 value must be declared for every takeoff, and not a range of speeds for this purpose. Therefore the speed V_1 must be chosen from this range thus obtained, *and must be adhered to*. Most operators like to use the highest value of V_1 that is permitted as this increases the chance of any engine failure that might take place doing so on the runway, so reducing the chances of taking a dead engine into the air, as is required should this failure take place after V_1.

Should the airport and runway, as used above, not have been at such a high altitude, and/or associated with such a high temperature not only would the TODA and EMDA intersection have produced a higher weight but the WAT limit would have been located to the right of this intersection, thus becoming non-limiting, and the TODA/EMDA interaction would have been valid and the limiting factor. Also should be noted the effect of TOD4 – the all-engines TOD. (The example worked is for a four-engined aircraft). This is the most usual effect with three- or four-engined aircraft, but is usually not limiting for twins.

As has been demonstrated, except in those cases where significant lengths of Clearway and Stopway exist, beyond the normal values – and bearing in mind that Clearway may not exceed 50% of TORA (UK Air Navigation (General) Regulations 1981, Para 5(3). FAR value is 33%.) – the most usual limitation is EMDA v TODA. However, WAT can very often exert its malign influence, most usually in the case of 'hot-and-high' airports and particularly where twin-engined aircraft are involved. The purpose of the WAT requirements is to ensure that in the case of an aircraft suffering an engine failure at, or after, V_1 its weight is such as to enable it to cross the screen at V_2 in the takeoff configuration and have a positive gradient of climb during the ensuing climb-out in the course of which the undercarriage is retracted and the takeoff climb element of the takeoff is completed and the en route stage takes over.

Engine Failure
Having so scheduled the takeoff performance so that the engine-failure case can be safely tolerated, and accepted (*in theory, anyway*), it remains for engine-failure throughout the en route element to be equally tolerated. However, here we are mainly concerned with terrain en route, and the ability to clear all obstacles throughout. For the terrain conditions en route an aircraft, with engine failure at or after V_1 must be able to safely clear all obstacles to the degree, as laid down by the applicable regulations. These will be gone into later. If the engine-out climb performance, as scheduled, does not permit a climb to a safe altitude then the aircraft must either land again at the airport of departure or do this at an alternative airport – whichever happens to be the most preferable course. In either case, the weight for landing must not exceed the Maximum Landing Weight, either structurally or as dictated by the performance requirements.

Should an engine fail en route, an aircraft may not be able to maintain its cruising Flight Level (i.e. Indicated Altitude÷100 with the altimeter sub-scale set to 1013.2 mb/29.92″ Hg e.g. 21 000 ft = FL210). As in the case of WAT and the climb-out, with an engine-out, the twin is most affected by this contingency. With the remaining engine(s) at maximum continuous power it may well drift down to an altitude where it can then maintain height. The contingency of an en route engine failure *must* be allowed for, and the engine-out stabilising altitude established for the whole route. The en route engine-out performance must be scheduled in the Flight Manual.

A few words on Performance scheduling at this point will be appropriate. All elements of flight performance are measured during an aircraft type's certification flight programme. During takeoff its Minimum Control Speed is established for a variety of conditions, all including an engine-failure (V_{MCA} *or* V_{MCG}). Minimum unstick speeds (V_{MU}) are established, as is Stalling Speed (V_S) for various configurations. Takeoff runway distances, likewise Landing, are measured, using sophisticated instruments, such as the kine theodolite (by triangulation) and telemetry. The flight testing will not normally be carried out at one airfield, either. Performance has to be scheduled for high altitude airports, hot airports, and airports possessing both characteristics. While measured performance at – say – one altitude (takeoff or landing case) may be extrapolated (i.e. calculated from the existing data), this is normally subject to prescribed limits, and to conservative factoring so as to include additional margins. Therefore it is normal to carry out further testing at hotter and higher airports – e.g. Madrid and/or Nairobi – so as to establish a wide range of conditions under which the scheduled performance has actually been measured.

Certificated Performance
Not only takeoff performance is measured, of course, and scheduled. The whole of each and every flight is governed by measured and approved, performance data. Following the takeoff comes the Net Flight Path, for example, which covers the segments from the screen to where the aircraft has both climbed and accelerated, up to the point at which it is aerodynamically 'cleaned up' – in other words, the safe flap retraction speed and height above the takeoff height. Normally this is 1500 ft above the runway screen. The en route Climb, with engine-out, is scheduled, as is the Cruise in such a form so as to provide the maximum altitude that may be attained, and *maintained,* with an engine failure. In appropriate cases the performance with two engines out is given. No such performance is given to the best of the author's knowledge and belief, in the case of a twin, for obvious reasons. With an engine-out en route, and the remaining engines at Maximum Continuous Power (MCP), all obstacles within 10 nm of Track must be cleared by at least 2000 ft either to Destination or Alternate. With two engines out, there is a time limit of 90 minutes, in still air. ANGRs section 3.4 and 5 refer.

Descent performance is not normally scheduled, but data is contained in the aircraft's Performance Manual, a document that contains flight planning data but which is not subject to Certification.

The Landing performance is scheduled, and is derived from measured flight performance in much the same way as in the Takeoff case. Normally the first item to be included is the Landing WAT performance. This is the scheduled performance to cover the aborted landing, or Missed Approach case, and gives the minimum acceptable *positive* climb performance, as a function of the weight of the aircraft when climbing away in a Missed Approach in the Landing configuration – i.e. gear down, flaps in the landing position. After the Landing WAT comes the establishment of the total Landing Distance Required from crossing the screen located at the threshold to the point at which the aircraft comes to a complete halt.

The Landing case, likewise the Takeoff, will be examined in detail later in this book, as most, if not all of the *scheduled* data contains

18   HANDBOOK OF AIRCRAFT PERFORMANCE

various safety additions, or 'pads', and these vary according to the certificating authority's philosophy and legislation. For example, is the Landing Distance Required scheduled with an engine-out and under what conditions, is the use of reverse thrust taken into account, and so on? But one thing is common – all scheduled performance is contained in a Flight Manual and this manual forms part of the aircraft's Certificate of Airworthiness; compliance is *mandatory*.

Finally, to close this generalised chapter, a short word as to what is held to be acceptable as regards risk during a flight. It is accepted that flight can never be 100% safe, and that there must be some tolerable level of risk. This is the normal *official* view, and not just that of the author. At the time of writing the maximum acceptable frequency of a fatal accident is set at one in 10 million flights, per hour (from the start of the takeoff to the end of the landing). This is expressed mathematically as 10^{-7}. Figure 2.2 shows how a flight can be divided up into three separate elements, viz: Takeoff and Climb; Cruise, Descent, Approach, and Landing. At the time of writing, the actual risk, in the first element, is believed to be higher than is acceptable. To be strictly correct, the word 'catastrophic' should be substituted for the word 'fatal'. The trouble is that definition of the risk is already difficult, and definition of the word 'catastrophic' becomes an almost impossible task. *One* fatality can be catastrophic to both the victim and near relatives. To attempt to define the risk we can start with the 10^{-7} element referred to in the previous paragraph; this refers to a target design airworthiness rate. This is the 'all causes' value, and includes the structure, systems, engines, etc. Only 15% of this is allowed against handling and performance faults, on the basis of 3×10^{-8} per flight, a third of which is allocated to handling, and the remainder to performance shortcomings. Time of flight enters

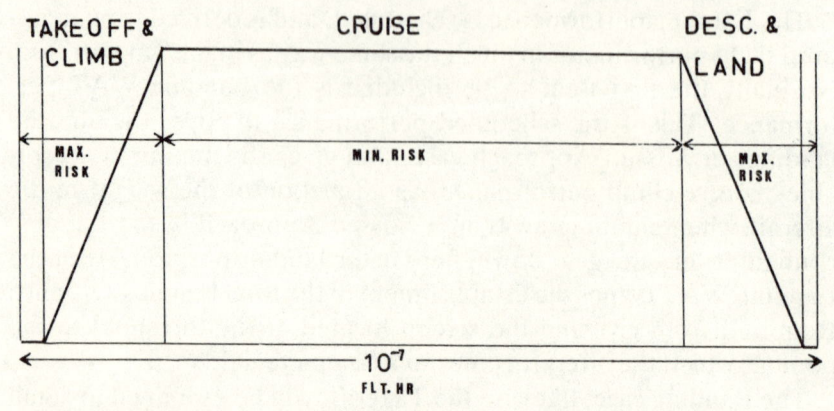

Fig. 2.2   The allocation of risks per flight hour

into the matter, and a long flight carries a greater element of risk than a short one, but this is not on a pro rata basis. Flight risks tend to be at their greatest during the takeoff and climb, and again at the approach and landing, the cruise being relatively safe in comparison. A formula used to attempt to quantify the total flight risk is: $R_{flight} = R_{hour}(0.6+0.4T)$, where R denotes Risk and T is Time.

Comment
It is understood that, in the early 1980s, accidents that had actually occurred showed that the 10^{-7} point was in fact being reached during the Takeoff and Climb sector alone, leaving the remainder of the flight profile without any risk 'cover'. A high proportion of the absorption of the acceptable risk element was almost certainly due to a number of takeoff accidents, and often these did not involve any engine failure. Two, in particular, were due to seriously degraded takeoff acceleration, being well below that required. All engines either were, *or appeared to be* operating normally. Neither need have happened had the applicable requirements regarding takeoff performance not taken the view that the Decision Point could be acceptably identified by the airspeed indicator. In the case of one of these accidents indications that not all was well were ignored, presumably on the grounds that as there had been no engine failure the regulations would take care of any possible problems. Both accidents were the subject of detailed Accident Investigation Reports, both took place in the USA, to US registered aircraft, and both are summarised in the Appendices to this book. The moral to the latter case is simple – if your engine instruments do not agree, something is wrong. Stop, and find out why.

3: Performance – Takeoff Requirements

The prime reason for establishing an aircraft's performance, and for recording this, is safety. Unless properly regulated the actual, measured, performance could be 'approved' at the whim of an aircraft's manufacturer. Such a situation would, of course, be quite unacceptable, human nature being what it is. Therefore the whole process of 'approval' must be placed in the hands of a totally impartial body having no vested interest in the aircraft at all. Such a body must evolve a set of standards for performance that apply to all types of aircraft originating from that body's area of jurisdiction. It is then the concern of the manufacturers to design and produce their aircraft so as to conform to the minimum applicable standards, at the very least – otherwise referred to as 'The Requirements'.

Up to now we have dealt with the various characteristics of the takeoff surface – i.e. the runway – and the generalised background to Performance Requirements. We now come to the more detailed exploration of the subject, and the legal, or regulatory, Requirements. So, first of all let us discuss what is meant by the word 'Requirements', and try to arrive at an acceptable definition in this connection. And as there are several sets of Requirements, issued by a number of States, this task becomes formidable indeed. Some of the various Requirements have much in common, while others choose to diverge.

Regulatory Bodies and Requirements

An examination of the overall Western world regulatory position as regards Airworthiness Performance Requirements shows that there are five main groupings, or divisions, and these are as follows. Firstly, there is the United Nations aviation agency – the International Civil Aviation Organisation, or ICAO as it is more usually referred to. ICAO has issued a set of Performance requirements, and most others are based on these. But the ICAO Requirements are advisory only, and carry no legal backing. The next, and probably the most important regulations are those issued by the USA Federal Aviation Administration, or FAA. For Transport Category aircraft, such as we are currently studying, the relevant requirements are known as Federal Aviation Regulations, Part 25, or FAR 25. The equivalent

UK document *was* British Civil Airworthiness Requirements, Section 'D', or BCARs Section 'D'. However, since 1979 BCARs Section 'D' has been replaced by the European Joint Airworthiness Requirements, Part 25, or JAR 25. And finally there are the Australian Director of Civil Aviation's Requirements or DCA. This latter legislation is believed by many to be the finest currently in use, but it is confined to Australia. It is worthy of note, though, that the safety record of Australian air transport is among the highest – if not *the* highest in the world.

BCARs Section 'D' continue in force for all transport aircraft certificated prior to the assumption of JAR 25 by the UK as its standard. Thus, as these types become obsolete, and leave the national Registers in the various countries in which they operate, so will BCARs Section 'D' slowly fade away, and their place will be taken over by JAR 25. The reasoning behind the assumption of JAR 25 by the various European states that subscribe to these regulations is mainly commercial, and is a reflection mainly of the way in which the European aircraft industry is forming into multi-national groups – e.g. Airbus Industrie. To have a common airworthiness, and performance code under such conditions is logical, while basing this code on FARs enables the Europeans to directly compete with the US aircraft industry. The main problem appears to be similar to that besetting the European Parliament, namely, national pride and failure to completely agree. Thus, while JARs often read paragraph for paragraph like FARs, individual states introduce their own national requirements, applicable only to the aircraft registered in that country. So, where JAR 25 should be, for best effect, a European norm, this is regrettably, not the case. And the UK is far from being backward in including its own national variants. However, for the purpose of this book, when JARs are mentioned these are *exclusive* of any national variants. To attempt to include those from other countries will, it is felt, only lead to confusion in the mind of the reader. Readers should refer to JAR 25 and any national variants that may affect them.

It would have been of interest to include information on the Australian DCA regulations, but space prohibits this. Therefore, this book will, unless stated to the contrary anywhere, only be dealing with performance matters covered by FAR 25, JAR 25, and BCARs Section 'D'.

The Takeoff
Let us first examine the takeoff, from the start of the takeoff run up to the point at which the aircraft crosses the imaginary 35 ft screen. Under the requirements of the three sets of regulations quoted in the

previous paragraph, there is a fairly high degree of commonality. However, FAR 25, *as implemented* is the odd-man-out on one major consideration, although this is far from apparent when reading this document. All the three requirements permit the actual use of reverse thrust in the accelerate-stop case, and for landing, and allow credit to be taken for this when scheduling the performance. An allowance must be made for a malfunction of the thrust reversers, and this is usually done by including the assumption that one engine is unserviceable, or that one of the thrust reversers is not functioning Minimum Control Speed (V_{MC}) must also be taken into account when asymmetric power is assumed, and this is checked during the flight test programme. But, while FAR 25 permits the assumption of reverse thrust for measuring the ASD required, and the LD required, and also permits its use in day-to-day operations, to the best of the author's knowledge and belief, the FAA have never permitted credit for reverse thrust to be taken in the scheduled performance. It may be that the FAA does not feel that the allowance for malfunction covers the situation enough. FARs states that credit for reverse thrust may be taken – or implies this, but has never given its formal approval for its inclusion in the scheduled performance in American Flight Manuals.

Let us examine the takeoff, as defined above, in more detail. A number of factors have to be accounted for in this phase of any flight, and the first of these is the somewhat loosely used 'Second-Segment' or WAT limitation, if any. (Strictly speaking, WAT covers the First and Second Segments, but the First Segment forms a comparatively small proportion of the total.) WAT, we will recall, is any limitation that may be exerted on the maximum takeoff weight from any particular runway as a result of the *airport's* altitude in feet amsl, and the ambient air temperature. This is dictated by the requirement that the aircraft, on takeoff, shall have a sufficiently positive gradient of climb while still in the takeoff configuration, and assuming that one engine has failed at, or after, V_1. Both JAR 25 and FAR 25 specify that, in these circumstances, and taking the distance from lift-off speed (V_{LOF}) to the point at which the undercarriage is fully retracted, all twin-engined aircraft must have a *positive* gradient of climb. Three-engined aircraft must have a gradient of climb not less than 0.3% greater than simply positive, while four-engined aircraft must show a 0.5% increment. This is the First Segment. For the Second Segment, which is almost invariably the more limiting of the two, due to the absence of ground effect, the required gradients of climb with undercarriage up and takeoff Flap are: 2.4% twins, 2.7% three-engined, and 3.0% for four-engined aircraft. Table 3.1, showing the differ-

PERFORMANCE – TAKEOFF REQUIREMENTS 23

ences between the takeoff assumptions of JARs, FARs, and BCARs is given at the end of this chapter, and gives appropriate references.

Note
Most, if not all *scheduled* performance data contains certain built-in safeguards, often referred to as 'padding', or 'an extra bit for Ma'. Needless to say, these last two expressions will not be found in any official publication! These safety features can either take the form of time, distance added – i.e. factoring up – or the diminishing of actual climb gradients. These last two are achieved by a simple mathematical correction. Basically the performance level that may be expected from a fleet of similar aircraft is established by actual measurement and calculation, and this is then referred to as being Gross Performance. This level of performance is then adjusted downward by given mathematical formulae so as to give a lower performance level, and this is referred to as being Net. Although Net and Gross are usually terms found in the Climb data, as scheduled, for the purposes of this book 'gross', in the lower case, will be used to denote measured, or established performance while 'net' will refer to scheduled performance. The Flight Manual contains the scheduled performance, and apart from some very early Flight Manuals, or Performance Schedules, it may be assumed that all the safety factors referred to have been included. Take, for example, the Wind Component correction grid. Here we are concerned with the value of the surface wind *component* that is blowing directly along the runway axis; the *wind velocity* is quite probably at an angle to the runway. The safety factor here, to allow for variations in the wind strength and direction, is that one may only assume 50% of a Headwind component, while one must assume that a Tailwind is blowing at 150% of its actual value. Incidentally, if the w/c grid in a Flight Manual has 'kinked' guidelines based on the Reference Line (which we shall see later) it means that the 50%/150% factor has already been taken into account; this is the normal practice, and has been so for many years. However, if the guidelines pass straight through the w/c grid then the correction has *not* been included. In which case check carefully that the various runway distances are gross or net – i.e. whether or not the prescribed increments are included. It is highly unlikely that this question will arise these days, but it is just possible in the case of an old type aircraft. (Most, if not all, Flight Manuals contain a chart that allows the actual wind direction and speed – i.e. the wind velocity – to be converted to the wind component blowing down the runway centre line.)

Weight Altitude and Temperature (WAT)

WAT is the first logical limit to examine, as there is little point in working out the runway and other limitations only to discover that these are invalidated by WAT. So check the maximum takeoff weight that is permitted by WAT (also loosely known as the Second segment Climb limit). If this is not the Maximum Structural Weight – i.e. the absolute maximum takeoff weight permitted by its Flight Manual – note the takeoff weight that is permitted by WAT. There are other limiting considerations, but these can be conveniently left until the runway limitation has been established. For example, there could be a Tyre Speed limit, but to check this we first of all need to know what the takeoff speeds V_1 and V_R are going to be. (In some aircraft, the effect of WAT can be ameliorated by converting excess runway available into a higher V_2, thereby increasing the initial climb gradients.)

In Chapter 1 the various elements that make up what is commonly known as the runway were defined. Now comes the time to use these so as to yield the best possible results, both as regards safety and commercial considerations. In Chapter 2 the takeoff performance requirements were described generally. Let us now take a specific case, starting with the assumption that WAT does *not* limit the takeoff weight. Takeoff Run Available (TORA), Takeoff Distance Available (TODA), Emergency Distance Available (EMDA) (also known as Accelerate Stop Distance in JARs and FARs (ASDA)), Airfield elevation, runway Slope, and Ambient Temperature are known, by promulgation, or, in the latter case, by measurement – as is the value of the Surface Wind. The Wind Component is obtained from the latter, by vector calculation. (The rather daunting sounding 'vector calculation' is in fact, normally achieved by the use of a pocket navigation computer).

Note

The illustration being explored *assumes* that an *ab initio* situation is the case. That is, the pilot is at an airport and is calculating his takeoff data from his aircraft's Flight Manual from scratch. In fact, in airline practice, and as required normally, by regulation, the pilot will have been provided with pre-calculated data for the airport and runway in question, leaving him to merely acquire, and to feed-in, the actual temperature and the wind component currently obtaining.

Before going into the detailed analysis of a specific takeoff case, with workings using Flight Manual-type charts, it will be beneficial if the applicable considerations are restated. In so doing, because of the amount of national variations that are involved, the basic principles only will be dealt with in this context. Many of the national differences can be found in tabular form in Table 3.1, at the end of this chapter.

First of all we have to consider WAT. This is to ensure that the aircraft has *at least* a positive rate of Climb after becoming airborne. While WAT covers the airborne elements of the takeoff from the screen height to the 400 ft height point, the overriding segment is after the undercarriage is retracted, but with takeoff flap selected up to the 400 ft height point, otherwise known as the Second Segment. The reason for this is that all the requirements under review introduce far more stringent *scheduled* climb gradients into the Second Segment – i.e. percentage 'add-ons' – than those for the first. Table 3.1 shows these increments in relation to the particular requirements listed.

At least there is more or less general agreement as regards WAT. It is when we come to the runway performance that we find the greatest number of variations, and it is not proposed to attempt to list these here. Again, reference to Table 3.1 will show how these differ, at least as regards the various mathematical 'add-ons'. The one thing that they all have in common is that one cannot regulate physical facts. That is to say, irrespective of the country involved, identical types of aircraft handled in an identical fashion on an identical runway in identical meteorological conditions at an identical airport altitude will, within the limits of an acceptable band of deviation (due to slight variations in power, aerodynamic Drag, etc.), all have identical runway performance. For example, an aircraft type weighing, say, 100 000 kg will, under the conditions listed above always take the same distance to accelerate to a given speed from a standing start. It will also always take similar values of deceleration distance to decelerate from this speed to a complete halt.

Runway Performance Requirements

After WAT let us remind ourselves of the runway-controlled outline requirements. These are:

1 The aircraft must be able to accelerate from a standing start and, with all engines operating, clear a screen (35 or 50 ft high) at the end of the Takeoff Distance Available (TODA), which includes a specified increment in the gross distance *required,* and with a screen speed (V_2) appropriate to the stalling speed. (Normally this increment is 15%; V_2 is *normally* 1.2 times V_S, but can be increased if desired in certain aircraft types to offset some of the WAT effect, if there is runway to spare.)

2 The aircraft must be able to accelerate from a standing start and then suffer engine-failure recognised at, or after, a pre-calculated Decision Speed or Decision Point. It must then still be capable of continuing accelerating, albeit at a reduced rate, so as to achieve V_2 at the 35 ft screen within the TODA.

3 The aircraft must be capable of accelerating from a standing start to an engine-failure point before or up to the Decision Speed and Point, V_1. From the actual speed at which the engine fails, V_{EF}, various time delays are introduced before it is assumed that the pilot *recognises, reacts, and rectifies* (i.e. takes rectification action). This is often referred to as the 'dither time'. The time delays vary from a simple 2 seconds under FAR 25 to a permutation under UK requirements, which not only puts in a 1 second delay between selection of each retarding device but also on how many crew members are contributing to the process. The aircraft must then be brought to a complete stop within the Accelerate Stop Distance Available (ASDA). No distance increments are involved in the scheduling process as regards ASD required.

4 The aircraft must be capable of becoming airborne within the Takeoff Run Available (TORA), including varying 'add-ons', and with allowance for engine failure. Table 3.1 gives details.

The basic rule that is common to all the requirements is this: it must be *assumed* that there will be an engine failure during the takeoff, at a speed known as V_{EF}. There is even agreement as to what to do, namely, if V_{EF} occurs before V_1 – abort the takeoff. If V_{EF} comes after V_1 – continue the takeoff. The choice of options is limited, because by law V_1 is the only point at which there is any choice. At V_1 the pilot may either continue, or abandon, the takeoff. With engine failure before V_1 he *must* stop, and after V_1 he *must* continue. Or if the pilot deliberately decides to continue the takeoff having recognised an engine failure before V_1, or elects to reject the takeoff (for any reason) after V_1, that pilot must be prepared to produce a very convincing case to justify the decision taken! It is operating rules rather than airworthiness, that requires V_1 to be specified before every takeoff *and to be observed*.

Comment

Here we have a weakness in the various requirements – the only contingency that is taken into account that will result in a reduction in performance levels, (other than the provision made for precipitation on the runway (see Table 3.1)) and which it is confidently assumed can be accepted as an 'acceptable risk', is that of engine failure during takeoff. No account is taken of any other factor that might result in the aircraft being at the wrong place on the runway for the speed attained. The enshrined principle seems to be – *if no engine failure is noted by the time V_1 is reached on the Airspeed Indicator everything must be all right.* But this is far from being the case. A brake defect – e.g. a binding brake – or a wrongly set engine thrust (EPR, or Engine Pressure Ratio) can both lead to seriously degraded acceleration, without any engine failure. In the Appendix section of this book, two classic fatal accidents have been analysed – there was no engine malfunction in either of them yet the aircraft failed to takeoff safely.

Misuse of V_1

Another point concerning V_1 is the fact that, properly calculated, it *must* be adhered to. To arbitrarily reduce the calculated V_1 can be a dangerous act. There are sound grounds for this fact, although many pilots believe that a reduced V_1 *increases* safety. Regrettably, the opposite is the case (except in the Wet Runway case – V_1 Wet. (See Chapter 4)). One airline operating what, in their day, were large four-engined jet aircraft even had the aircraft manufacturer warn them about this practice. The instance involved a long, but 'humped' runway. Not being able to see beyond the very approximately, midway point, some pilots doubted the aircraft's stopping capability from V_1 – which normally came up shortly before the peak of the runway's hump. Had they been able to see the distance remaining from the V_1 point, they would probably have seen no problem. But, because of this Human Factor, V_1 as calculated was reduced on the flight deck without any technical backing.

Consider the facts. Firstly, V_1, once selected or declared, becomes a legally binding value. If engine failure occurs and is recognised at any point *up to* V_1 there is no problem – if the value V_1 is taken 'from the book'. The dangerous – or potentially dangerous, situation arises when V_1 is artificially reduced. (If an engine fails at a value just below the *legal* V_1 it may also involve V_{MCG}, because V_1 may not be less than V_{MCG}.) Now let us move on to the second main consideration. The takeoff acceleration is based on all-engines operating up to the V_{EF} point associated with V_1. If V_{EF} occurs *after* V_1 one engine will be out, and the takeoff *must*, by regulation, be continued. However, from the V_{EF} point the rate of acceleration will start to decay until it reaches the engine-out level. What happens when V_1 is illegally reduced is simply that the required takeoff element with an engine-out is increased in terms of distance. In other words, the scheduled distance to the screen is going to be exceeded in the case of a reduced

V_1. If the runway involved is TODA limited (or just sufficient) the aircraft using a reduced V_1 will reach the end of the TODA *below* the screen height, the actual height depending on how low V_1 is reduced below the correct value. If there are obstacles involved in the engine-out climb the reduced V_1 could well cause them to penetrate the flight path, with possibly fatal results. To take an absurd, but quite appropriate illustration, think of a case where V_1 is reduced to say, 20 kt. If the critical engine fails after this, the takeoff *must* be continued, even if V_{EF} were to be as low as say, 40 kt. In fact, the major part of the takeoff would be subject to the engine-out level. Given a long enough runway the aircraft would probably unstick and eventually drag itself into the air – and into the obstacles (if any).

This question is raised because the airline involved that had pilots who used this practice was using the airport with the 'humped' runway very frequently, and there were significant obstacles beyond the screen position. It was established beyond reasonable doubt by the aircraft manufacturer's aerodynamics and performance department that the level of reduction of V_1 being practised by some of the pilots failed to provide obstacle clearance in the case of V_{EF} being reached shortly after the illegal V_1.

Note
The airline involved ceased operating some years ago.

Worked Example
Having covered a few safety considerations let us now go into a full takeoff calculation, using an Approved Flight Manual. The aircraft involved in this example will be a BAe 146-100. This has been selected because it was the first aircraft to be certificated under JAR 25, and it will be the subject of all Performance calculations and examples throughout this book, unless an occasional example is used that involves another aircraft. If so, these few examples will be clearly identified.

Note
Production considerations concerning this book prohibit the reproduction of all the appropriate charts from the Flight Manual. All appropriate charts are referred to, however. In addition, if another aircraft type is considered certain other charts could be involved, and these will also be mentioned as examples.

The Flight Manual charts reproduced have been redrawn to suit production considerations, although the layout has not been altered. They must **not** be used operationally, due to possible drawing errors or variations.

Given Data:

Airport Elevation	6000 ft (Pressure Altitude)
Ambient Temperature	30°C
Takeoff Run	1870 m
Takeoff Distance	1920 m
Accelerate-Stop Distance	1900 m
Slope	0.2% Down (Start elevation 6050 ft, ASD end elevation 6030 ft Both amsl)
Wind Component	5 kt Headwind (Reported)

The example chosen shows that we have a typical 'hot and high' airfield, and the runway is not over long. The Ambient Temperature is high for the altitude, and this all adds up to a potentially limiting situation. Let us go through the charts and see what the end result is.

Proceeding in logical sequence, we first ascertain the effects of the temperature and weight combination. Taking the chart given in Fig. 3.1, we find that we can obtain three different weight limitations as a result. This is because of the three flap settings available for takeoff, viz: 30°, 24°, and 18°. Flaps are useful things for takeoff, but care must be taken to use the optimum setting. A high deflection gives improved Lift, and shortens the ground run, but the concomitant Drag adversely affects the Climb. A low deflection reduces Lift, resulting in a longer ground run, but also reduces Drag, thus improving the Climb gradient. Here we are looking at the 'Second Segment' Climb, or WAT. Enter Fig. 3.1 at the airport altitude, 6000 ft and move across to intercept the 30°C temperature line. Now move downwards vertically to the Reference Line, and follow the guide line backwards (or upwards again) to 30° Flap. Move vertically down to the Weight scale and discover the Weight, limited by the Second Segment Climb requirement, 30 200 kg. This applies to the 30° Flap setting. Now repeat the process, this time for 24° Flap. This is also the Reference Line, so proceed straight through vertically to the Weight scale and read the 24° Flap limit, 33 250 kg. Repeat again for 18° Flap and reading from the Reference Line along the guide line find the Weight 35 400 kg. This gives the highest WAT limited weight.

Next we go to Fig. 3.2, a somewhat complex-looking chart. Enter from the left with the TODA 1920 m and move horizontally across to the Slope correction grid Reference Line. Follow the guide line to the 0.2% Downhill Slope, and then across horizontally to the Wind correction grid Reference Line. From here follow the guide lines to the

30 HANDBOOK OF AIRCRAFT PERFORMANCE

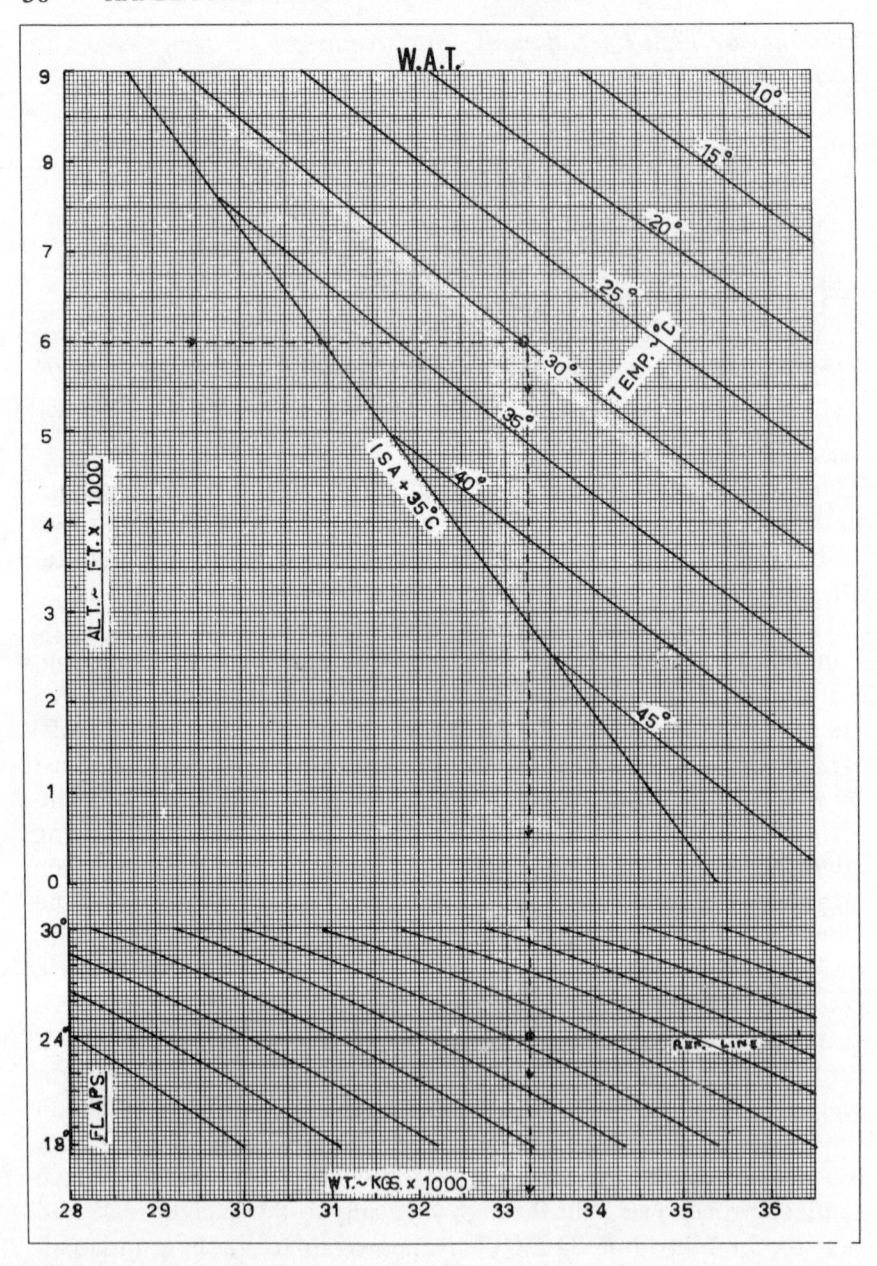

Fig. 3.1 WAT – the variation in takeoff weight for different flap settings due to the effects of Altitude and Temperature

5 kt Headwind component and then move horizontally across the 'D' and $V_1:V_R$ web grid. Draw in this line with a sharp pencil. Now repeat the process, but entering with ASDA 1900 m and working vertically. Note where the vertical line crosses the horizontal TOD line;

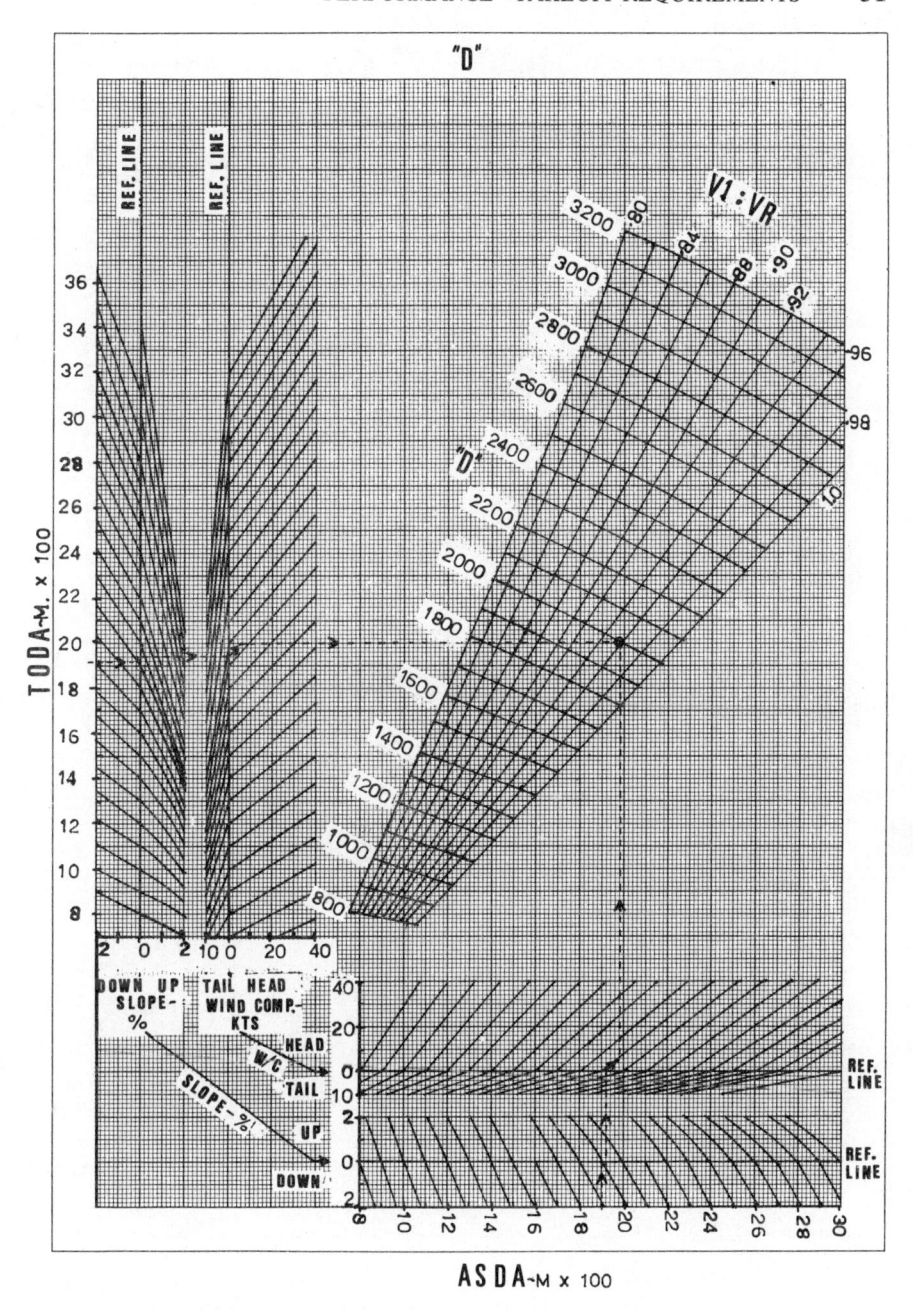

Fig. 3.2 The derivation of an equivalent Balanced Field from TODA and ASDA

in the case being considered it intersects on the 'D' line – i.e. the Equivalent Balanced Field Length – 2000 m while the $V_1:V_R$ is shown to be 0.96. The whole example is shown in Fig. 3.2 by means of dotted lines.

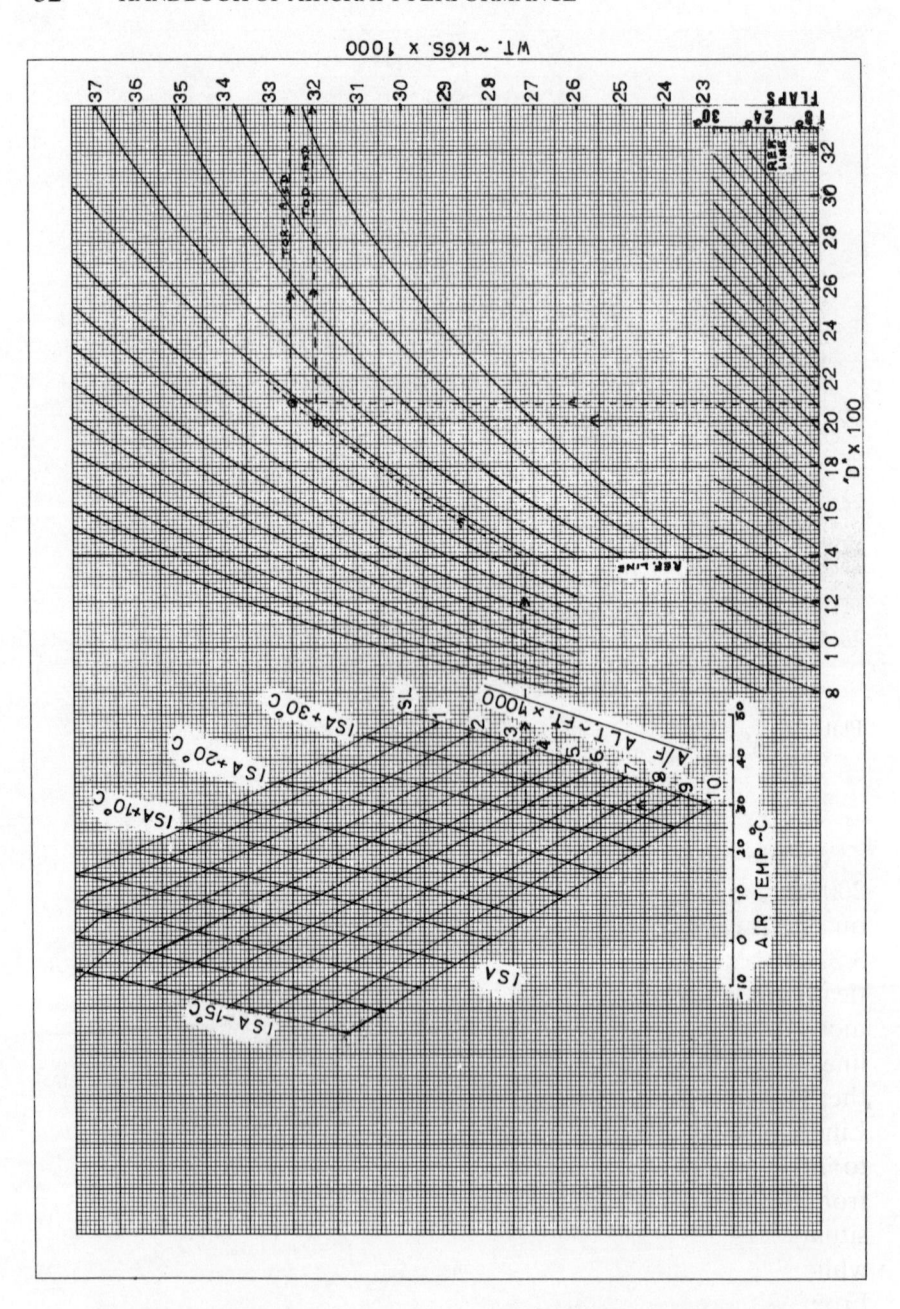

Fig. 3.3 The derivation of Regulated Takeoff Weight from an Equivalent Balanced Field value. Here TODA and ASDA exert the more stringent limit

PERFORMANCE – TAKEOFF REQUIREMENTS 33

Plate 1 Just after V_{LOF}; BAe 146 nears V_2. (*Photograph courtesy of British Aerospace*)

We now have an Equivalent Balanced Field Length *available* of 2000 m, and a $V_1 : V_R$ ratio of 0.96. From this we must first of all find out what weight the runway will permit for takeoff. Referring to Fig. 3.3, and entering with the Ambient Temperature 30°C, we move vertically to the Altitude grid and the 6000 ft line. From this point we move horizontally right to the 'D' Reference line, using the guide lines to enable us to locate a 'D' curve. Pencil this in. Now enter with the 'D' value 2000 and move to the Flap correction grid Reference Line. Follow the guide lines to the 30° Flap point, then move upwards to intersect the 'D' line that has been pencilled in. Read to the right from this intersection, the Weight 33 100 kg. If we check the 18° Flap situation we find that 'D' = 2000 gives a takeoff Weight of 30 500 kg, while WAT limits at 35 400 kg. The 24° Flap 'D' limit is 32 000 kg. From all these weights there is only one that can be used, namely the 24° Flap 'D' limited weight. 18° Flap gives us a WAT limited weight of 35 400 kg, with a 'D' limit of 30 500 kg. 24° Flap gives a WAT limited weight of 33 250 kg, but with 'D' limiting further at 32 000 kg, while 30° Flap yields 30 200 kg WAT, and 33 100 kg 'D' limits. Hence, the optimum Regulated TOW (RTOW) is 32 000 kg, using 24° Flap, for TODA and ASDA.

We have now established a Limiting Weight and $V_1:V_R$ based on the engine-out TOD and ASD requirement, for the 24° Flap setting. We must now check further to ascertain the effects of TORA, both for the engine-out and the all-engines cases. Taking the engine-out case first we apply the runway data to a very similar Flight Manual chart to the TOD v ASD, as shown in Fig. 3.2. (This TOR v ASD chart is not presented, due to editorial considerations, but in it TORA is substituted for TODA.) TORA is 1870 m; proceed exactly as before in the case of Fig. 3.2, and find a 'D' value of 2080, and a $V_1:V_R$ of 0.94. Applying this new 'D' value (it used to be known as the 'R' value in some earlier Flight Manuals, such as those for the Viscount and BAC 1-11) to Fig. 3.3 gives us a RTOW of 32 500 kg. But TODA v ASDA only gives a weight of 32 000 kg, and is therefore the more limiting.

Now we must check on the all-engines case, using TORA and TODA. TORA gives a 'D' value of 2130 (Flaps 24°), and TODA gives a 'D' value of 2000. From the foregoing workings we have found that TODA and ASDA limits with a 'D' value of 2000, and this is less than the all-engines 'D' of 2130. It is still the more limiting, and therefore still valid. The all-engines TODA gives a similar 'D' to that obtained from the engine-out TODA v ASDA case presented in Fig. 3.2.

Table 3.2 Takeoff Weight for altitude and runway.

Example Airfield Limiting Factor	RTOW (kgs) for engine out and all-engines Flap Settings		
	30°	24°	18°
WAT	30 200 L	33 250 X	35 400 X
TODA/ASDA*	33 100 X	32 000 L	30 500 X
TORA/ASDA*	33 700 X	32 500 X	31 100 X
TORA all-eng.	34 300 X	32 800 X	31 000 X
TODA do.	33 100 X	32 000 L	30 120 L

Notes
1. Lowest weight in each column is RTOW for the Flap Setting.
   Highest weight of these three values thus extracted is the optimum Maximum TOW.
2. The higher the Flap Setting the *greater* the weight for the runway distances, etc.
   The higher the Flap Setting the *lower* the weight for WAT.

* = one engine out   L = Limiting Weight.   X = non-valid weight.

PERFORMANCE – TAKEOFF REQUIREMENTS

Therefore, for the example so far worked, 'D' = 2000 and $V_1:V_R$ is 0.96, which gives a RTOW of 32 000 kg. Table 3.2 shows results for all Flap settings, which clearly indicates that 24° Flap is the optimum setting *for this example and aircraft type*. (The principle holds good for other aircraft types although the numbers will, of course, certainly vary.)

Having now obtained an apparent RTOW we must refer to another chart in the Flight Manual that has not been reproduced. This covers Brake Energy Limits, and shows that there are no limits at 32 000 kg due to Brake Energy Requirements. Also to be checked, in the case of this aircraft, is the matter of any Tyre Speed Limits. Even if the aircraft is fitted with 160 mph tyres there is no limit (the standard 190 mph tyres are totally unlimiting). So we have nearly, but not quite, finished our calculation; one thing more has to be done, and once more the appropriate chart is not reproduced – we need to obtain the Speeds V_1, V_R and V_2.

To Go or Not to Go

The latter is a simple process. In the case of the BAe 146-100, and in most other cases, the known RTOW controls both V_R and V_2. We also have the $V_1:V_R$ ratio 0.96. Thus, entering Fig. 3.4 with Temperature we move to airport altitude and thence to the weight line 32 000 kg at both the V_R and V_2 correction grids. 32 000 kg gives us a V_R of 108 kt. IAS, and a V_2 of 115 kt. Now refer to Fig. 3.5, and enter the V_R scale with 108 kt. Move vertically upwards to intersect the 0.96 $V_1:V_R$ line, then move left horizontally to read the V_1 value 103.5 kt.

So, we know that the RTOW, or Maximum permissible takeoff weight is 32 000 kg, and that the V_1 for this weight and ASDA is 103.5 kt, while the V_R is 108 kt, and V_2 is 115 kt. But, suppose that the takeoff weight is, in fact, less than the RTOW. Are these speeds valid? The answer is no, but they are erring on the safe side. Suppose that the *actual* TOW is 30 000 kg. From Fig. 3.3, enter from the Weight scale with 30 000 kg, and move horizontally left to intercept the valid 'D' curve. From the intersection move vertically downwards to read a 'D' value required of 1720. Now go to Fig. 3.2 and locate the 'D' = 1720 line. Where this line intercepts the TOD and ASD corrected lines, as shown in the example, are two $V_1:V_R$ ratios, and both are outside the web grid. So we can use any choice of $V_1:V_R$ between these two extremes – i.e. from 0.80 to 1.0. From the Flight Manual we find that V_R is 105 kt and V_2 is 111.5 kt. Using Fig. 3.5 we find that for the V_R value of 105 kt the ratio 0.80 produces a V_1 of 84 kt and ratio 1.0 gives a V_1 of 105 kt. V_1 *must* be chosen, and specified, as a single speed between these two values, by regulation.

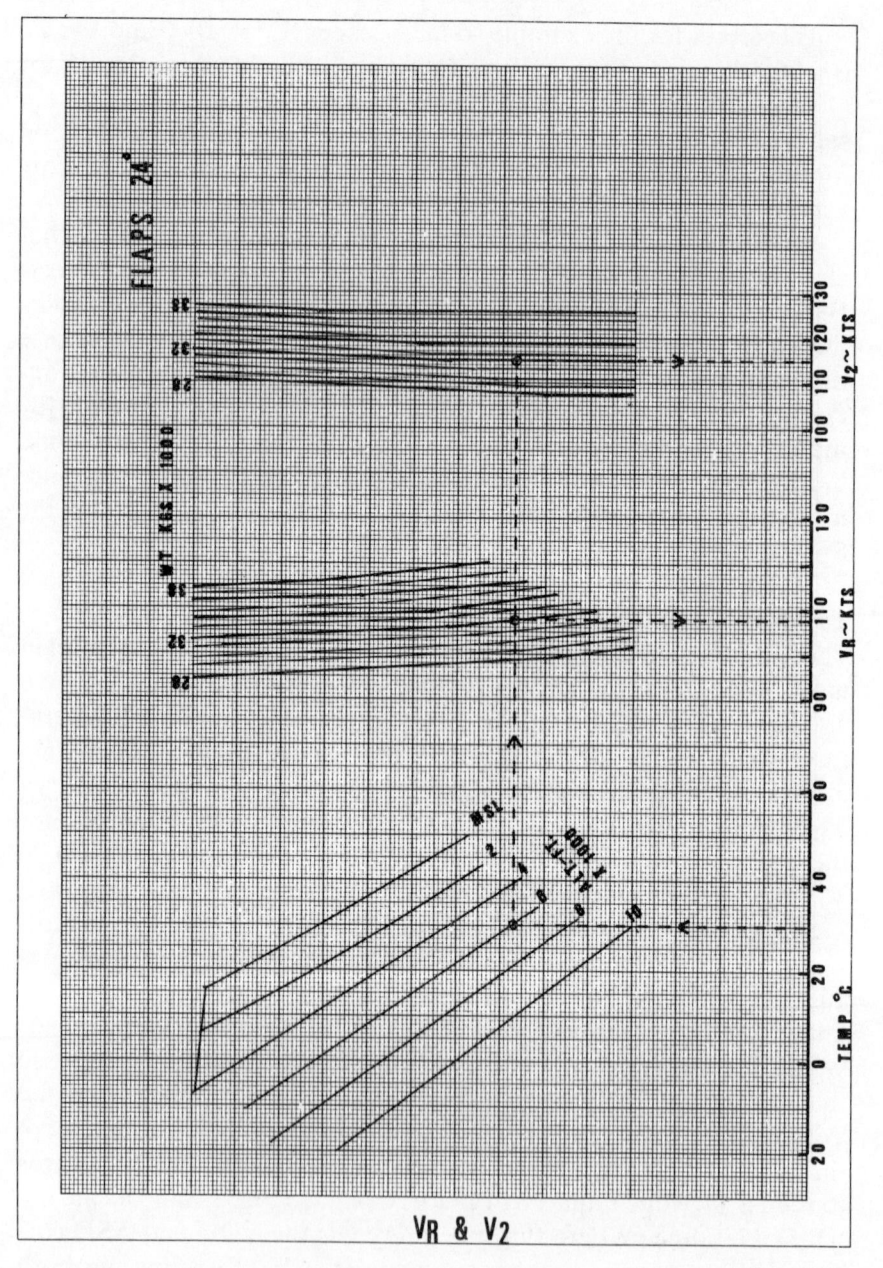

Fig. 3.4 The derivation of V_R and V_2 from altitude and temperature

The figures that have been used to illustrate the example worked are, as explained earlier, taken from the JAR Flight Manual for the BAe 146-100. However, the format is still very similar to most mod-

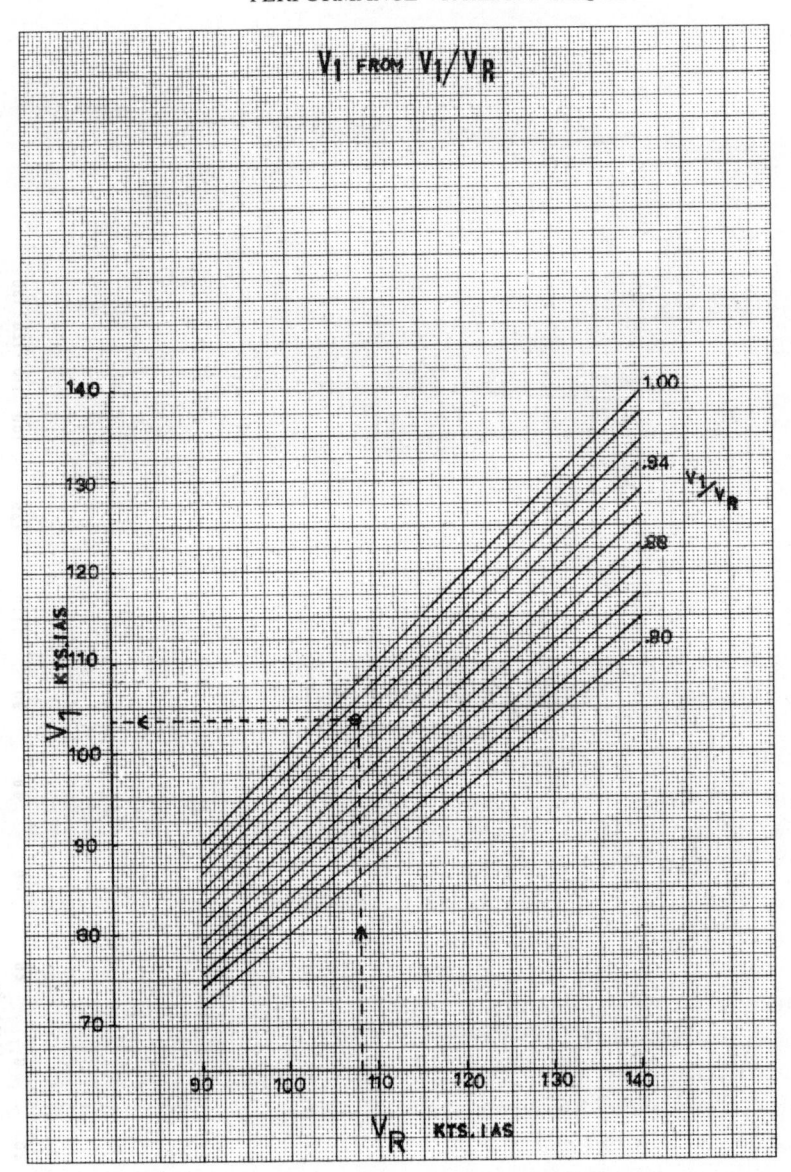

Fig. 3.5 The derivation of V_1 from the $V_1 : V_R$ ratio

ern Flight Manuals, and if one type can be used, it is not difficult to 'read' another. The Flight Manuals for the Lockheed L-1011, the Fokker F28, and F27 are, for example, all very similar, as are those for the Viscount and the BAC 1-11. There are certain differences between each, mainly as a result of the aircraft's characteristics and the

Plate 2 Rotation V_R – a BAe 146 assumes the altitude for transition from ground roll to flight. (*Photograph courtesy of British Aerospace*)

manufacturer's performance scheduling. In the case of twin-engined aircraft there are, as far as is known, no all-engines operating charts to check, as the all-engines case is less limiting and therefore the one engine out TOR and TOD performance is built into the 'D' charts, and it is not normally necessary for these parameters to be checked. This, by the way, is due to the fact that a 50% loss of power is involved that outweighs the 15% all-engines factor. The TOD, engine-out does not carry this 15% factor.

In all modern Flight Manuals – i.e. those going back 30 years or so – all the various 'add-ons' and factoring are included in the charts, and these can be used by applying the published, or reported, values. Normally the Flight Manual text will make this clear. But, just take a quick glance at Fig. 3.2 again, and specifically at the Wind Component correction grid. Note how the guidelines 'dog-leg' at the Reference Line. This is because of the requirement that 50% be added to a Tailwind, while only 50% of a Headwind may be used; the 'doglegging' indicates that this has been carried out in the structure of the chart. But, if you see wind correction guide lines passing through the Reference Line smoothly, be on your guard – it may be that the TOR and TOD all-engines 'add-ons' have also not been applied.

Finally, to end this chapter, let us look at the *absolute* Limitations for this aircraft. The maximum permitted weight for Takeoff, due to structural considerations, is 37 308 kg, and this may never be exceeded *in any circumstances*. There is also a varying Maximum TOW, due to WAT that results in an operating limit of ISA+35°C, and this is shown on the WAT chart in Fig. 3.1.

Table 3.1 Brief comparison of the main elements of the various requirements.

Phase	FAR 25	JAR 25	(G) JAR 25	BCARs, Section D
WAT	*FAR 25.121 (a)* 1. V_{LOF} and the undercarriage retraction completed point, without ground effect but with takeoff Flap. Minimum Gradient of Climb must be: Positive for twins 0.3% minimum for three-engined aircraft 0.5% for four-engined aircraft All with one engine out from V_{EF} and taken from the V_{LOF} point. 2. From the undercarriage-up point without ground effect. Minimum Gradient of Climb must be not less than: 2.4% for twins 2.7% for three-engined aircraft 3.0% for four-engined aircraft. All with one engine out from V_{EF}, u/c Up, Flaps at takeoff setting, all up to the 400 ft Height point.	*JAF 25.121* As for FAR 25.121.	*(G) JAR 25.121* As for FAR 25.121.	*Subsection D-2, Ch D2-4, para 2* 1. As for FAR 25 *but* assuming Maximum Contingency Power (MCP). 2. Where MCP *not* automatic, Minimum Climb Gradient not less than: -1.0% twins -0.7% for three-engined aircraft 0.5% for four-engined aircraft All with remaining engine(s) at Maximum takeoff power. 3. Second Segment Climb, one engine out, u/c Up, Flaps at takeoff setting. Minimum Gradient of Climb not less than: 2.4% for twins, 2.7% for three-engined aircraft 3.0% for four-engined aircraft 4. At 400 ft, all engines at Maximum takeoff power, Gross Gradient of Climb not less than 5.0%

Table 3.1 cont'd

Phase	FAR 25	JAR 25	(G) JAR 25	BCARs, Section D
ASD	*FAR 25.109* The greater of: 1. (Dist. from start, with all engines, to V_{EF}) + (Dist. V_{EF} to V_1, with acceleration continued for 2 seconds after V_1) + (Dist. to stop from end of 2 seconds point), with engine failure from the V_{EF} point *or* 2. (Dist. from start to V_1, +2 seconds, all-engines) + (Dist. to stop from end of 2 seconds point).	*JAR 25.109* As for FAR 25.109.	*(G) JAR 25.109* The greatest of: 1. (Dist. (all-engines) from start to V_{EF}, *Dry* runway) + (Dist. V_{EF} to V_1, *Dry* runway, with acceleration continued for 2 seconds after V_1, *Dry* runway) + (Dist. to stop from end of 2 seconds point) *or* 2. (Dist. from start to V_{EF}), *Wet* runway, all-engines) + (Dist. V_{EF} to V_1, *Wet* runway, with acceleration continued for 2 seconds after V_1, *Wet* runway) + (Dist. to stop from end of 2 seconds point, *Wet* runway) *or* 3. (Dist. from start to V_1, *Dry* runway + 2 seconds, all-engines after V_1) + (Dist. to stop from end of 2 seconds point) *or*	*BCARs D2-3.7.1* The greater of: 1. (Gross Dist. from start to V_{EF}, *Dry* runway) + (Gross Dist. from V_{EF} to V_1, *Dry* runway) + (Gross dist. to stop, one engine out, *Dry* runway, with *all* available means of retardation used) *or* 2. (Gross dist., all-engines from start to V_{EF} point, *Wet* runway) + (Dist. from V_{EF} point to V_1, *Wet* runway, one engine out) + (Gross dist. to stop, one engine out from V_1 point, *Wet* runway, with *all* means of retardation used).

TOD	FAR 25.113 The greater of:	JAR 25.113 The greater of:	(G) JAR 25.113 The greatest of:	BCARs D 2-3 Para 6 The greatest of:
	1. Dist. from start to 35 ft height point, with engine failure at V_{EF} or 2. 115% of Dist. from start to 35 ft height point, all-engines.	1. As for FAR 25.113 or 2. As for FAR 25.113 or 3. Dist. as in (2) above, but with precipitation on runway, depth 150% of nominal average depth. *Ground* acceleration in this precipitation. (JAR 25.113 (a) (3)	1. Dist. from start to 35 ft height point with engine failure at V_{EF} point, *Dry* runway or 2. Dist. from start to 15 ft height point, with V_2 before 35 ft height point, *Wet* runway, one engine out or 3. 115% of dist. from start to the 35 ft height point, with V_3 before 400 ft height point, all-engines ((G) JAR 25.107 (g) or 4. As for JAR 25.113 (a) (3).	1. 115% of Gross dist. from start to V_R point, and thence to 35 ft height point and V_2, all-engines, *Dry* runway or 2. Gross Dist. from start to V_{EF}, then accelerate from this point to V_1 point, with one engine out, then dist. to 35 ft height point at V_2 min, *Dry* runway or 3. Gross dist. all-engines, from start to V_{EF} point, thence to V_R with one engine out, thence to V_2 point, with a height of 15 ft *Wet* runway. *Note:* For *Dry* runway the greater of 1 and 2 applies, while for *Wet* runway the greatest of 1, 2 or 3 applies.

4. (Dist. from start to V_1, *Wet* runway, +2 seconds all-engines)+(Dist. to stop from end of 2 seconds point, *Wet* runway).

Phase	FAR 25	JAR 25	(G) JAR 25	BCARs, Section D
TOR	*FAR 25.113 (b)* The greater of:	*JAR 25.113 (b)* The greater of:	*(G) JAR 25.113 (b)* The greatest of:	*BCARs D-2.5* The greater of:
	1. Dist. from start to mid-point between V_{LOF} point and 35 ft height point, one engine out	1. As for FAR 25	1. Dist. from start to mid-point between V_{LOF} point and 35 ft height point, one engine out, *Dry* runway	1. (115% of gross dist. from start to V_{LOF} point) + (⅓ gross dist. from V_{LOF} point to 35 ft height point at V_2), all-engines, *Wet* runway
	or		or	or
	2. 115% of dist. from start to mid-point between V_{LOF} point and 35 ft height point, all-engines operating.	2. As for FAR 25	2. Dist. from start to V_{LOF} point, with engine out at V_{EF}, V_1 as for *Wet* runway	2. (Gross dist. from start to V_{LOF} point) + (⅓ of gross dist. from V_{LOF} point to 35 ft height point at V_2, one engine out), *Wet* runway
		or	or	or
		3. Dist. as 2 above, but with precipitation on runway, depth 150% of nominal average depth. *Ground* acceleration in this precipitation.	3. 115% of dist. from start to mid-point between V_{LOF} point 35 ft height point, V_2, with V_3 before 400 ft height point, all-engines	3. Gross dist. from start to V_{EF},* thence, with one engine out to become airborne. Technique as for TOD *Wet* runway
			or	or
			4. Dist. as in 3 above, but with precipitation on runway, depth 150% of nominal average depth. *Ground* acceleration in this precipitation.	4. For a *Dry* runway the greater distance as obtained in 1 and 2 above, but without references to *Wet* runway.

Note: All engine-out cases assume that the Critical engine has failed.

*The actual TOR *Wet* is *measured* with engine failure, to the airborne point. However, the *technique* required is the same as the TOD, with engine failure, for a *Wet* runway (V_2 at 15 ft screen). (See BCARs D2-6. 1(c).)

4: Supplementary Takeoff Considerations

The runway itself, with all its possible physical permutations, does not alone complete the requirements covering the takeoff. Unfortunately it is not quite as simple as that. But if safety is to be considered, as it *must* be, then matters must be taken further. Not only safety gains thereby, there are also strong commercial factors that benefit by good scheduling of performance considerations. For example, excess runway available may be converted into higher V_2 values, and this speed increase can be converted into steeper first and second flight path segments, with a concomitant reduction on WAT limits where these intrude. Excess runway may also be used to reduce the engine takeoff thrust that is selected and this in turn results in an improvement in engine life (e.g. in time between overhauls – TBO – or in condition at overhaul). Then such things as brake efficiency and tyre speed have to be taken into account, and so must any precipitation on the runway.

In Chapter 3 we dealt with the effects of aerodrome Altitude, Temperature, and Runway dimensions on takeoff performance. It could be thought that these factors alone are enough to more than adequately cover the takeoff consideration. Unfortunately, this is not the case, and we must now examine other takeoff considerations which both amplify those already spelled out, and which can also affect the results.

As explained in Chapter 3, WAT always takes precedence over runway when establishing Regulated Take Off Weight (RTOW). This is because the Initial Segment of the Takeoff Flight Path (which is looked at in more detail later) requires a *minimum* gradient of climb that is positive, with one engine out. This ranges from anything that is more than 0° – i.e. positive for twins; up to 0.5% for four-engined aircraft. The Second Segment calls for a climb gradient of not less than 2.4% for twins, 2.7% for tri-jets and 3% for four-engined aircraft. The WAT limited weight will ensure this. But, if the runway-limited weight is less than the WAT limit then this becomes the limiting weight for takeoff. Conversely, if the runway-limited weight is higher than the WAT limit then a takeoff using the runway-limited weight would almost certainly result in the required climb gradient *not* being met, whether due to WAT or Flight Path (see Chapter 5), and this could well result in a failure to meet any obstacle clearance requirements. It makes no difference if there are no obstacles as for example, in the case where the runway ends with nothing but the sea beyond. Unless the climb gradient is positive a continued takeoff could result in a 'ditching'. However, where obstacles are present, the Takeoff Flight Path can override WAT limits.

Flap Settings

Flap settings are important when considering WAT and, as previously mentioned, WAT limits are paramount. A high flap setting gives a shorter ground roll, due to increased Lift, but a reduced climb gradient, due to Drag. A low flap setting gives a longer ground run, due to a lower Lift value, and a higher climb gradient, due to lower Drag. Many aircraft have a 0°–10° takeoff flap setting for takeoff for making use of long runways and offsetting any WAT limits. In such cases the runway RTOW can be the highest, but the longer run and higher V_1 can exert higher airframe and engine stresses. So, where the *required* RTOW permits, it can be preferable to use at least *some* flap (or the next notch up from the minimum scheduled setting), as long as the 'Second Segment' climb requirement is met in full (see Fig. 4.1).

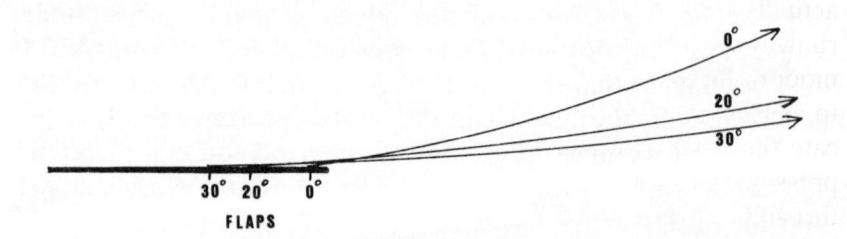

Fig. 4.1 The effects of flap settings on distance to liftoff and gradient of climb

Reduced Thrust Takeoffs

Another factor that can adversely affect the ground roll requirement is the Rolling Start technique. This is where an aircraft taxies on to the runway and then lines up for takeoff without stopping; takeoff power is then applied with the aircraft still moving. Thus takeoff power is not applied from a standing start. In the early generation of turbine-powered aircraft this technique could increase the total ground roll by up to 10%, due to the comparatively slow response, or 'spool-up' of the gas turbine as opposed to the piston engine. This would mean that the aircraft was consuming runway at a relatively low rate of acceleration until takeoff power was finally attained. In fact, some Flight Manuals contained some guidance as to the extra ground roll required when using this technique. The normal procedure is to run up to the required thrust (EPR) against the brakes, and then release these when required EPR is attained.

Yet, where excess runway is available, there is a benefit in the use of this technique – *if specifically permitted* – in terms of brake life, and to a lesser extent, tyres. There might be some fuel saving as well, depending upon the engine characteristics. It should be borne in mind that by the time the aircraft reaches the runway Holding Point – i.e. the point set aside for an aircraft to come to a halt before turning on to the runway – it may well have had a long taxi run from the Terminal. This could mean that if the brakes have been used in the taxi-out element to any extent, they could be hot. If so, they will become hotter still if the aircraft is lined-up and then halted before takeoff. However, this is the normal technique, and is scheduled as being appropriate to the takeoff Flight Manual charts. It is certainly no more hazardous than a Rolling Start, any benefits of which are mainly economic.

Another economic technique is that of Reduced, or Flexible thrust for takeoff. In this procedure the engines are not opened up to maximum available takeoff power but rather only to the power actually needed to achieve the required heights and speeds within the runway distances available, WAT, and obstacle clearance limits. In modern jet engines, jet engine power settings are frequently referred to as Engine Pressure Ratios, or EPR, and there are gauges to indicate the EPR that has been selected, or applied. This ratio is Compressor end Pressure : Intake Pressure. The calculation of reduced thrust for a takeoff is relatively simple and straightforward, and involves the assumption of an *assumed* ambient temperature (Tflex) when excess runway (or takeoff path distance) is available. This assumed temperature will be higher than the ambient value, and EPR is directly related to ambient air temperature. So the basic procedure for the calculation of a reduced thrust EPR is simply to find out, for actual all-up weight and reported wind component, the ambient temperature at which, for runway, WAT, and takeoff path obstacle clearance requirements, the *actual* weight becomes limited. The lowest ambient temperature that limits, from all these considerations, is the limiting temperature for our purpose. For example, if the *actual* weight is, say, 32 000 kg, first find the ambient temperature at which the runway limits the RTOW to this weight. Let us say that this is 30°C. Next check the WAT limit – say, 32°C. Then, finally, the flight path for obstacle clearance (which is looked at in more detail in a later chapter) compliance – say 33°C. The lowest temperature that limits the RTOW to 32 000 kg is therefore 30°C, and it is this temperature that we must use to establish the EPR that would be available. Thus we establish a value of EPR for an *assumed,* or Tflex, temperature, while the actual ambient temperature may be only – say – 20°C.

For this takeoff the EPR for 30°C is therefore set by the throttles, and the takeoff is carried out using this value. Because this 'artificial' takeoff power is based on the use of all the runway distances, as defined earlier, the aircraft should cross the screen at the end of the TOD available. In fact this is not the case, and herein lies a safety margin (this being one of two). The *actual* ambient air temperature is, in fact, 20°C, and this means that the takeoff is being carried out in cooler, denser, air than that being assumed. Therefore the screen point will, or should, be reached before the end of the TODA, because the achieved performance level is, in fact, better than that being assumed as being appropriate to 30°C. The second safety factor is essentially that the takeoff thrust selected is less than that available. Therefore, in an emergency, there is more power available in reserve. But, bearing in mind that the achieved acceleration as a result of reduced thrust is lower than that for the case in which maximum thrust for the actual temperature produces – i.e. if reduced thrust was not being used for the takeoff, care must be taken when selecting full power that the V_{MC} requirements are fully met. For example, if an engine fails before V_1 during a reduced thrust takeoff, care must be taken that the procedure does not call for the application of full power on the remaining engine(s) that would result in a situation where asymmetric power causes control problems, either on the ground (V_{MCG}) or when airborne (V_{MCA}).

Contaminated Runways

A cautionary note – the use of reduced thrust for takeoff is *prohibited* when operating from wet, or contaminated, runways. The trouble is, not surprisingly, that the sheer complexity and diversity of these conditions have led to a commensurate complexity in the Regulations, from all sources as shown in Table 3.1. There are even discrepancies, it would appear, between the various Regulations and the data contained in the various Flight Manuals, and these are supposed to reflect the regulatory requirements. So, this is a further complication in an already complex matter. The main point of complexity is the number of ways in which this very real operational problem is being tackled. For example, FAR 25 is somewhat vague about the whole thing and basically requires that the takeoff data in the Flight Manual be presented for a hard, dry runway (FAR 25.105 (c)1). But, in con-

SUPPLEMENTARY TAKEOFF CONSIDERATIONS 47

sidering the ASD case FAR 25.109 (d) requires *correction factors* for those cases where the Stopway surface is substantially different from that of the runway (TOR). These corrections include the surface characteristics *of the Stopway, together with rain, snow, and ice.* But these corrections are not quantified *in the Regulations.*

JAR 25 is essentially equally vague as regards the ASD; (JAR 25.109 (d) follows FAR 25.109 (d) precisely). But, as regards TOR and TOD, JAR 25.113 is far more demanding and quantifies the accountability for precipitation (JAR 113 (a) (3)). The correction required is that the ground acceleration must be assumed to take place in precipitation having an *assumed* depth of 150% of the nominal average depth. Further, it is *advised* that an absolute depth of 3 mm be the maximum permitted and that takeoffs should be *prohibited* where this depth is exceeded. (ACJ 25.113 (a) (3) 1.) ACJs are *advisory* only. See also ACJ 25.1533 (b), JAR 25.1533 (b), and JAR 25.1091(d) (2). Summed up, these Requirements call for limiting precipitation depths to be scheduled and contained in the Flight Manual. Even more detail regarding the *establishment* of the effects of precipitation is to be found in JAR 25 – the Specific Gravity of the precipitation is defined as ranging between 0.2 and 1.0 *(Estimated Data)*. Also the Water Equivalent Depth (WED) should not exceed 15 mm. WED is the equivalent depth of water corresponding to the precipitation depth and SG. But, JAR 25×131 to 133 provides for the correction to V_1 in conditions of icy, snowy, slushy, or just plain wet, runways.

Further *advisory* requirements are that the estimated Aquaplaning Speed, which may be approximately calculated by the formula $9\sqrt{p}$, where p = the tyre pressure in pounds per square inch (psi), should be factored by 1.10. There are also advisory notes regarding the estimated undercarriage displacement Drag (factor by 1.30), and the estimated spray Drag (factor by 1.80). But these are essentially certification guides so that the appropriate corrections can be presented in Flight Manuals. There is some relaxation when *measured,* as opposed to *estimated* data is available.

(G) JAR 25.113 – i.e. the JAR applicable to British requirements – introduces a somewhat different approach. Here we have a value of V_1 that is appropriate to a *Wet* runway, associated with a reduction of the Screen Height to 15 ft. (*Note*: this is an *approved* V_1 reduction and does not apply to dry runway routine cases.) (G) JAR 25.113 (a) (4) also deals with the UK requirements for precipitation-covered runways. These follow those set out in JAR 25.113 (a) (3).

BCARs Section D (D2-3) introduces yet further differences, although to be fair these preceded the introduction of JARs. Firstly, two values of V_1 were introduced, these being either for Dry – V_1 Dry, or Wet – V_1 Wet, conditions. The gross acceleration time between these two values of V_1 may not exceed 4 seconds, with all engines operating. The TOR requirement is the greater of

1. *Dry runway* 1.15×distance to V_{LOF}+⅓ of the distance from the V_{LOF} point to the 35 ft screen, all-engines, or
2. *Dry runway* Distance to V_{LOF}+⅓ of the distance from the V_{LOF} point to the 35 ft screen, with one engine out, or
3. *Wet runway* Distance to V_{EF}, thence to V_{LOF}, V_R, and then to the 15 ft screen height. See Table 3.1 (TOR Wet). 'In a manner consistent with the achievement of a speed not less than Takeoff Safety Speed at 35 ft. . . .'. In other words, V_2 at the 35 ft screen.

The TOD requirement is phrased somewhat similarly, but with an engine-out element replacing the ⅓ distance from the V_{LOF} point to the 35 ft screen. Thus we have to take *the greater of:*

1. *Dry runway* 1.15×gross distance, all-engines, to V_R and thence to the 35 ft screen at V_2, or
2. *Dry runway* The gross distance, all-engines, to V_{EF}, and then to V_R, and V_2 at the 35 ft screen, or
3. *Wet runway* The gross distance to V_{EF}, all-engines, then an engine-out acceleration distance to V_R, thence to the 15 ft screen as in the TOR case.

The wet ASD case is based on the greater of:

1. the all-engines gross distance to V_{EF} (*Dry runway*)+the gross distance to V_1 (*Dry runway*)+the gross distance to stop from V_1 on a dry, hard, surface, using all available means of retardation or
2. gross distance, all-engines, to a V_{EF} corresponding to a *Wet* V_1 (*Wet runway*)+the gross distance, one engine out, from V_{EF} to V_1 (*Wet runway*)+the gross distance to stop, one engine out, from V_1 (*Wet runway*) on the 'Reference Wet Hard Surface' using all available means of retardation. (D2-3.3 to 3.7 refers.)

'Reference Wet Hard Surface' is, in fact, a norm. It was based on a wet, hard surface on which a specially-built measuring trailer towed by a vehicle would measure the ambient braking force coefficient. The value thus obtained varied with groundspeed, in knots. (It was deleted from JAR 25 in March 1987 by Amendment No. 87/1) BCAR D2-2, Appendix 1, 1.6 refers.

Note
In those cases where correction values for icy runways are provided

SUPPLEMENTARY TAKEOFF CONSIDERATIONS

(BCARs Section D), in some instances these can result in V_1 becoming invalidated, due to the fact that the engine-out requirement for the continued takeoff cannot be met, and also could be less than V_{MCG}. Under these circumstances a risk may have to be accepted between values V_1 Maximum and V_1 Wet.

Table 4.1 gives the required reduction, in knots, to convert the V_1 Dry, as obtained using Fig. 3.4, into a V_1 appropriate to a Wet runway. Having established V_1 Wet it is necessary to check through a revised $V_1:V_R$ that the 'D' value available is sufficient to meet the ratio V_1Wet$:V_R$. (UK only BAe 146-100.)

Table 4.1.

Flaps°	\'D\' (in metres)					
	1000	1500	2000	2500	3000	3500
18°	11	9	8	7	6	5
24°	10	8	7	6	5	
30°	9	7	6	5		

Wet, or precipitation-covered, runway operating data is contained, in one form or another, in most Flight Manuals, usually in the form of correcting data to apply to the Dry case.

Reverting to JAR 25, Section 2 ACJ 25X131 introduces the advisory scheduling of ASD for runways having a very low braking coefficient – i.e. not *exceeding* 0.05, or in fact, an icy runway. Using all available means of retardation, only 50% of the *available* reverse thrust may be assumed. ACJ2 5X132 also includes data for the scheduling of Drag in precipitation exceeding 3 mm, with a braking coefficient not exceeding 0.05.

When considering wet, icy, or precipitation-covered runways, the concept remains whereby a reduced V_1 associated with a reduced 15 ft screen height is used, as previously mentioned. But reference should be made to JAR 25X131–JAR 25X133; these three Requirements do, in fact, *require* data to be determined or established for slippery or precipitation-covered runways, and also for a Wet V_1 to be determined.

Note
Normally JAR numbers correspond with FAR numbers – e.g. JAR 25.109 is the same as FAR 25.109. *New* JAR material, *not* contained in FARs but placed numerically in the FAR/JAR numbering system, is designated by the letter X – e.g. JAR 25X131.

50 HANDBOOK OF AIRCRAFT PERFORMANCE

Precipitation – Some Figures

In the case of our main example aircraft, namely the BAe 146-100, data is provided in compliance with JAR 25X131-133. At the time of writing the US FAA has issued Notice of Proposed Rule Making (NPRM) that will require Precipitation accountability, in addition to the Wet Runway case. We are now considering the Contaminated Runway, which is declared to exist when either Standing Water, Slush, Wet Snow, or Dry Snow accretions exceed 3 mm in depth. The density of Slush and Snow is defined as follows:

Slush: 0.85 kg per litre
Wet Snow: 0.4 kg per litre
Dry Snow: 0.2 kg per litre.

Note how the density decreases when the wetness (for want of a better word) also decreases.

In our example, absolute Limitations are laid down, apart from the introduction of corrections to TODA and TORA. These Limitations

Plate 3   BAe 146 landing on contaminated runway at Aspen, Colorado. Altitude some 8000 ft. (*Photograph courtesy of British Aerospace*)

are two in number; the first is applicable to Standing Water, Slush, or Wet Snow, and must not be deeper than 12.5 mm. The second is applicable to Dry Snow (see above) and allows a maximum depth of 50 mm. The operating configuration of the aircraft stipulates that the takeoff Flap setting must be 30° (to obtain maximum lift, irrespective of aerodynamic Drag, and doubtless to gain the greatest benefit from ground effect), and Reduced Thrust may *not* be used. A rolling takeoff is recommended for slippery surfaces, because of the reduced directional control available at low speeds due to this being derived solely from nosewheel steering. Once the rudder becomes effective, with increased speed, so does directional control improve.

Performance data for Contaminated Runways accepts a degree of increased risk. The most important thing to note is that the all-engines *only* situation is allowed for. Also to be noted is that the V_1 Wet does not apply, and the concept of an aborted takeoff is also abandoned. It must be accepted that, particularly in the case of very low coefficients of friction, it will probably be impossible to stop, unless there is substantial ASD available in excess of that required for a Wet runway. Even at speeds down to V_1 Wet – 50 kt an overrun could be likely.

Figure 4.2 shows how the TODA is corrected to give an *equivalent* Dry runway TODA. The whole of the TOD *available* is used to obtain the correction, and the process is simple. Enter the chart with the TODA, proceed to the reported depth of precipitation, and read off the equivalent TODA Dry. A similar chart is used to correct the TORA to its Dry equivalent. It is assumed that the reported precipitation depth is true, and continuous; the chart depth equals 1.5×reported depth. That is to say, the calculation is based on 1.5× the depth of actual precipitation and this increment is included in the chart figures.

These correction charts are only valid for Standing Water, Slush, or Wet Snow. When the runway contamination consists of Dry Snow only 0.25 of the actual depth is used to address the chart. One other important point; it will be recalled that the all-engines case for TOD and TOR is subject to an increment of ×1.15 – i.e. the Takeoff Distance Required (TODR) and (TORR) Takeoff Run Required is multiplied by this figure. Because of this, the normal 'D' value may well become invalid, and a check must be made to see if this is, in fact, the case when using the Contaminated Runway correction. This is accomplished by obtaining the corrected 'D' value as described above, and then using this value as though it were the actual TODA or TORA for a normal Dry runway, using the chart portrayed in Fig. 3.2.

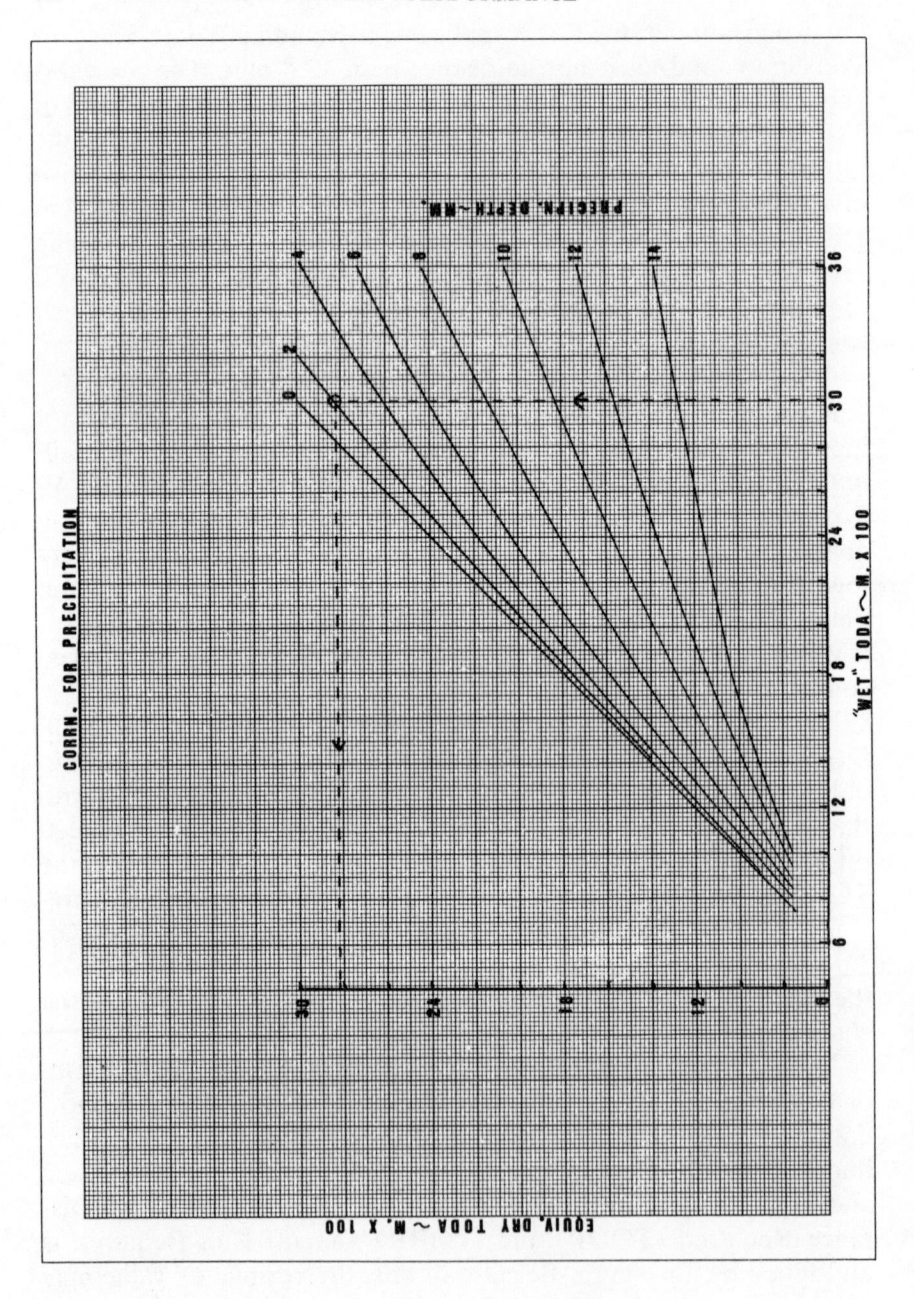

Fig. 4.2 Contaminated runways – how depth of precipitation reduces the equivalent TODA

SUPPLEMENTARY TAKEOFF CONSIDERATIONS 53

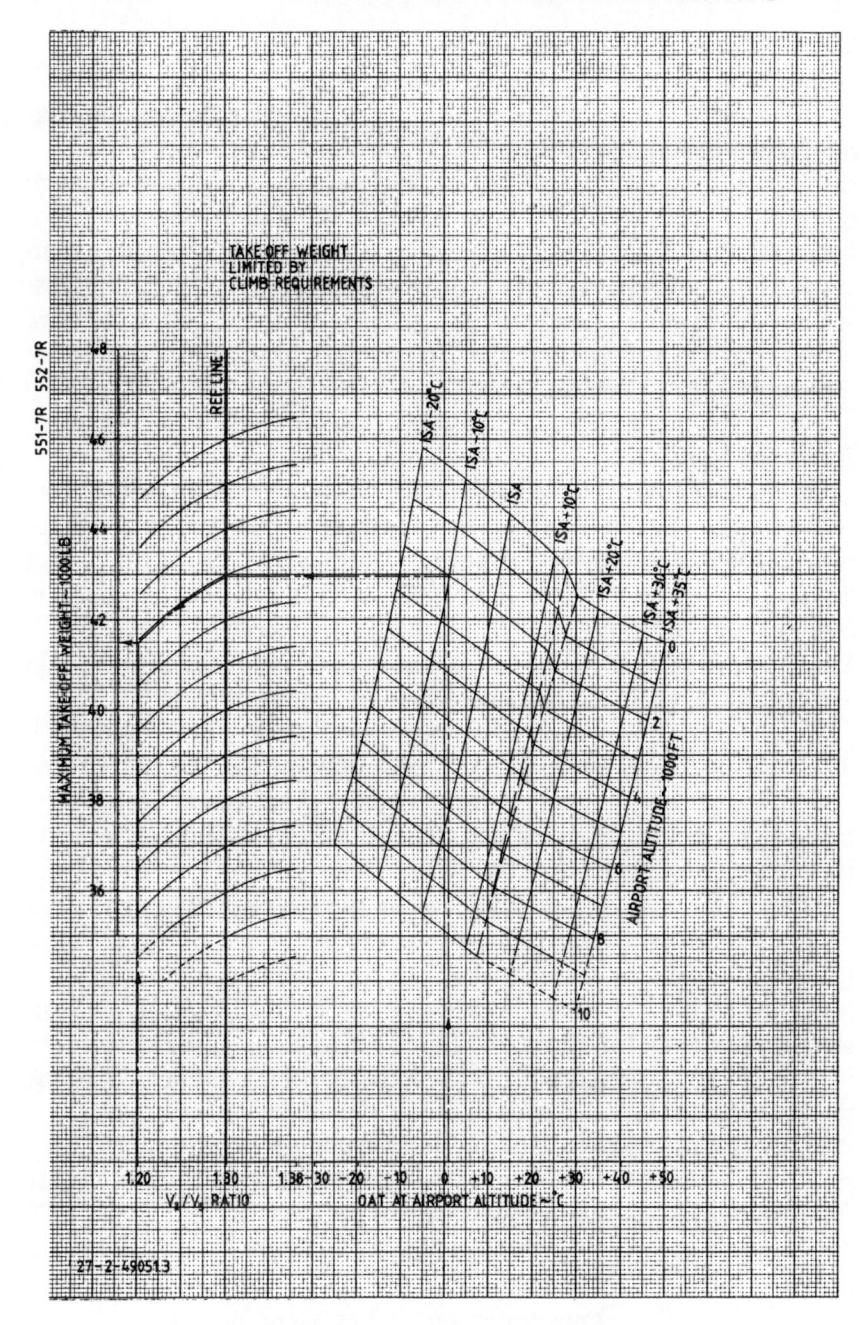

Fig. 4.3   F-27, Wet takeoff power, 16.5° flap

V_2 'Overspeed' Techniques

Mention has been made of fully approved techniques that make use of excess runway availability to alleviate the effect of the Second Segment (WAT) requirement on RTOW. We have seen how the higher the takeoff Flap setting the less limiting becomes the runway distance requirement, while WAT becomes more limiting. By changing to a lower Flap setting the WAT effects become less pronounced (or can even disappear), but instead a more restricting runway limit emerges. An answer in such cases is to use a Flap setting that results in *some* excess runway over that required and then to set about a technique to reduce the effect of WAT.

Increased V_2 or V_R

From the foregoing it can be seen that, by changing Flap setting, one restriction can be played off against another, and an optimum Limitation or RTOW established. But this is a somewhat crude method of 'optimising' the RTOW, relying as it does on merely changing the Flap setting. A typical, and far more effective method of playing off Flap v Runway is that used by Fokker in the case of the F27 and F28 aircraft (and, to be fair, also by Sud Aviation in the case of the Caravelle; other manufacturers, more recently, have followed suit). The basic technique is achieved by 'paper engineering', and for many years this became a significant factor in making the Hot-and-High performance of the F27 so much better than its contemporaries – i.e. the twin-turboprop types. (See Fig. 4.3.)

The technique used, and scheduled in the F27 and F28 Flight Manuals, is to convert excess runway into a higher value of V_2 (or V_R in the case of the F28). As normally V_2 minimum is based on 1.2×stalling speed (V_S) in the takeoff configuration, the technique under consideration allows for excess ASD *available* to be converted into a higher V_2 (V_2 maximum), normally limited to 1.3 V_S, but 1.38 V_S for the F27. When this technique is used there must always be sufficient ASD available to take care of the aborted takeoff requirement for the resulting increase of V_1 (as the value of V_1 is linked to V_2 (and V_R) by the ASDA through the ratio $V_1 : V_R$, or $V_1 : V_2$ in the case of the F27; any increase in V_R or V_2 will bring about an increase in V_1 as appropriate to the ratio). The maximum value of V_1 is limited to a $V_1 : V_R$, or $V_1 : V_2$, of 1.0; V_1 may not exceed either V_R or V_2.

If we take the case of the F28-3000, by way of example, a continuously variable V_2, within the permissible range $V_S \times 1.2$ to 1.3, is scheduled for the 6° Flap setting, which is the optimum setting available for making use of this technique, aerodynamically. V_2, it will be recalled, is a function of *Weight*, while the ratio $V_1 : V_R$ (and thus V_2)

is a function of ASDA. Likewise *Climb* is a function of speed. Therefore the Second Segment climb will vary with the value of V_2 being used. Weight also plays a part in climb, and a higher climb gradient will permit a higher weight, *assuming that the higher gradient is reduced to the minimum required* as a result of a weight increase. Thus the WAT limit *decreases* (there is less *limit* – i.e. the weight is higher) with increased V_2 (above $1.2 \times V_S$, and not exceeding $1.3 \times V_S$), but because of the concomitant increase in V_1 the ASD *requirement* increases. This does, admittedly, further complicate the calculation of the optimum takeoff weight and speeds but it does pay dividends where temperature and altitude values are high. Put simply, the calculation is really only a question of plotting the change in WAT limited RTOW for at least three values of V_2, these being chosen quite arbitrarily, against a similar number of ASDA values. Figure 4.4 shows how both runway limits (or 'field length') and climb gradients vary with V_2. The author is indebted to Fokker, from whose F28-3000 Flight Manual this sketch has been taken, and very slightly modified.

Acceleration and Stopping Distances

Incidentally, leaving the subject aside now of V_2 variations, it is worth reflecting on another element of 'paper engineering' that is contained in both the F27 and F28 Flight Manuals. Although this matter is still – regrettably – somewhat academic at present, these Manuals contain data giving distance required to (a) attain V_1, and (b) stop from V_1 following upon an abandoned takeoff. This is of interest in that the *Speed* V_1 is associated directly with a quantified *Distance*, under the actual conditions obtaining for each takeoff, viz: Weight, Temperature (ambient), Altitude (pressure), Slope (runway), and Wind Component (reported). But the question must be asked – how does the pilot relate distance consumed to Speed (IAS) attained in practice? The present answer must be – he (or she) does not, or cannot. On certain runways – mainly in the USA, and on military airfields – runway Marker Boards are provided at stated intervals, and these can give a very approximate idea. Yet the whole basis of takeoff (and also Landing) performance is the correct relationship being achieved between Speed and Distance. This whole question will be commented on and discussed in some detail, at a later stage in this book; it is also referred to in Chapter 2.

To end this chapter, and to end the consideration of the takeoff up to the V_2 point (35 ft Screen point), there are two more matters that have to be taken into account and allowed for. These are (a) Brake

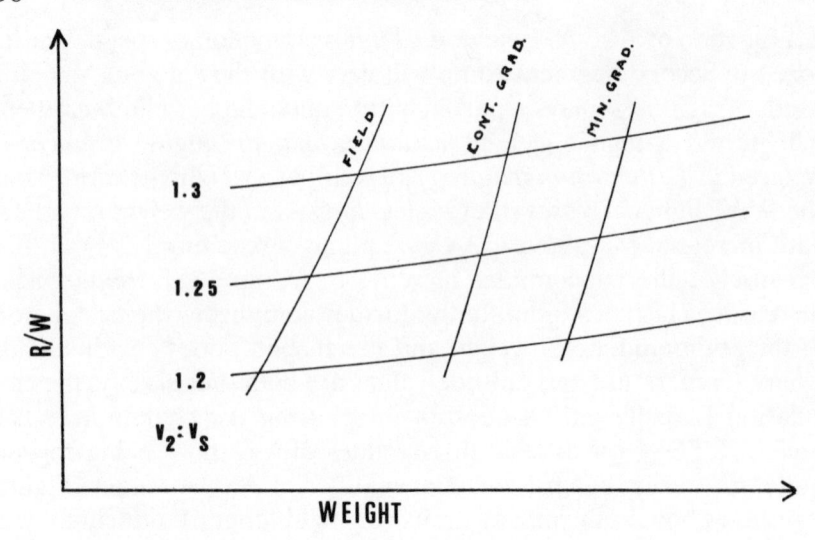

Fig. 4.4 How an increased V_2 value can, runway length permitting, reduce some takeoff weight restrictions

Energy Limit, and (b) Tyre Speed Limit. Neither calls for complex calculations.

Brake Energy Limits
The Brake Energy Limit is a speed, V_{MBE}, and is the maximum runway speed (IAS) from which the brakes can bring the aircraft to a stop. V_{MBE} *can* affect V_1, as V_1 may not exceed V_{MBE}. Should the lowest value of V_1 exceed V_{MBE} the only available correction is by means of weight reduction until $V_1 = V_{MBE}$. Normally V_{MBE} only becomes a problem in the (usually) unlikely circumstances of a downhill takeoff with a Tailwind component. V_{MBE} for takeoff is only concerned with the deceleration element of a rejected takeoff, where the brakes have to be capable (even allowing for the use of all other available means of deceleration or retardation) of stopping the aircraft from V_1. V_{MBE} is a straightforward function of Weight, Altitude (pressure), OAT, Slope, and Wind Component. It is Newtonian in that the consideration is simply the deceleration of a given mass from a given speed. A (relatively) simple chart is included in most modern Flight Manuals to enable V_{MBE} to be checked.

Tyre Speed Limits
The Tyre Speed Limit is a straight mechanical limit on the rotational speed of the aircraft's tyres, expressed, unusually, in miles per hour

SUPPLEMENTARY TAKEOFF CONSIDERATIONS   57

as opposed to knots. It is based on the ability of the tyres structurally to accept the highest ground operating speed likely to be encountered during takeoff – i.e. normally V_{LOF}. Although airfield Altitude (pressure), and OAT enter into the check for any limit imposed by Maximum Tyre Speed it should be borne in mind that there will be a specified tyre pressure that is not a part of the *performance* requirements. However, atmospheric pressure, and OAT, outside the tyre can affect the tyre's pressure due to expansion of the tyre itself and also the inflating vapour. Therefore it will normally be only the 'hot and high' airfields that will introduce any limits.

Bear in mind also that, for all other performance purposes, we are dealing in knots, and thus lower numerical values than would be the case were mph to be the value. For example, a V_{LOF} of 210 kt approximates to 240 mph.

Where Tyre Speed Limits are frequently encountered, and at the same time Maximum RTOWs are commercially required, the only remedy is for tyres having a higher speed rating to be fitted. As a general rule the higher the speed rating of a tyre the higher is the required tyre pressure and the higher the tyre pressure the smaller the tyre 'footprint'. Reduction of the total 'footprint' area of an aircraft's tyres – i.e. the total contact area of all tyres with the runway – means a higher weight distribution across the total 'footprint' area. The runway must be of a sufficient strength structurally to accept the weight per square inch, or cm, in contact with the runway for each tyre. This is known as the Isolated Single Wheel Load (ISWL) which is expressed in terms of weight. Runway Bearing Strengths are promulgated (normally) with other relevant details – e.g. length – and usually this information is given as Load Classification Number (LCN), or sometimes Maximum All up Weight (auw). LCN is the more normal; both are functions of the runway structure.

Which type of route pattern an airline uses, can influence the tyre speed rating in that the runways to be served may, through their respective bearing strength characteristics, dictate the type of tyres to be fitted to the airline's fleet. Thus, where the airports are relatively small, regional, and simple, the user-operators may be obliged to fit low pressure tyres to meet LCN, or Maximum auw bearing strength limits. And low pressure tyres may well impose RTOW limits through tyre speed restrictions. So the question therefore becomes basically one of economics, and resolution of the question – which imposes the more stringent limits, high pressure tyres and RTOW losses due to bearing strength limits, or low pressure tyres and possible tyre speed limits?

In the case of the BAe 146-100 the use of standard, 190 mph tyres causes no Tyre Speed limits, and therefore no data using such tyres are provided in the Flight Manual, other than a statement to the effect that 190 mph tyres are non-limiting. A simple chart is provided to enable the mandatory checks to be carried out when 160 mph tyres are fitted, to ensure that RTOWs meet tyre speed limits. Higher flap settings can often exert lower weight restrictions, due to increased Lift resulting in shorter takeoff runs, and lower V_{LOF} values in consequence.

5: The Takeoff Flight Path

After each takeoff the next item that must be taken into account is the climb up to the point where the aircraft is 'clean'. That is to say, when the undercarriage is up and the flaps are in the en route position. This phase of each flight can take the form of a number of climb profiles; in many cases these considerations are not significant. But when obstacles are in evidence the Flight Path can often become the significant limiting factor affecting the takeoff.

In the opinion of the author the takeoff Obstacle Clearance requirements, or Takeoff Flight Path, (BCARs still refer to the Net Flight Path) are prescribed as some form of penance – or should be, anyway! Yet they are very necessary, in that their purpose is to ensure that, after the takeoff, all obstacles in the extended centreline of the runway plus a defined, but diverging, area on either side, are cleared by a prescribed 35 ft vertically. The real trouble is simply, the number of options open regarding the procedure to be followed and the almost total lack of definition as to exactly what comprises the Net Flight Path. In most cases an 'envelope' is defined, and performance must be scheduled that lies wholly within this envelope. In the case of, for example, V_2, the various considerations are precisely defined for each set of regulations being followed. This is not generally the case as regards the Net Flight Path. As a measure of the flexibility of the situation, only the now replaced BCARs even use the expression 'Net'. Instead there are Takeoff Paths, and Takeoff Flight Paths, and this terminology extends throughout FAR 25 and JAR 25, including (G) JAR 25.

Generally speaking, the three regulatory requirements cited above vary little; BCARs Section D is the odd man out, but is much more specific. In the course of this chapter we will attempt to deal with the Net Flight Path in a similar fashion to that used in the case of the takeoff to the Screen height, as described in Chapters 3 and 4.

FAR 25
FAR 25.111 defines the Takeoff Path as being the flight profile from a standing start up to the point at which an aircraft (*a*) attains a height of 1500 ft above the takeoff surface, or (*b*) completes the transition to the en route configuration (in terms of altitude), at a speed of *not less*

than 1.25 V_S, with one engine out – *whichever is the highest altitude*. The assumption must always be made that an engine fails at V_{EF}, as described in Chapter 3, followed by an acceleration to V_2. V_{EF} may *not* be less than V_1 for the purposes of the Takeoff Path.

The Takeoff Safety Speed V_2 must be attained *before* the 35 ft Screen. As the distance before the screen, for this purpose, is not specified we can interpret the requirement to be that V_2 must be attained by the Screen, and certainly not after. At *all times* during the Takeoff Path the gradient of climb must be positive. The speed V_2 must be held, as closely as possible, up to a height of not less than 400 ft above the takeoff surface. Also, the speed may not be less than V_2, although it may exceed this value.

From the point at which the height of 400 ft is attained the climb gradient *available* must be not less than 1.2% for twins, 1.5% for tri-jets, and 1.7% for four-engined aircraft. (The context 'jets' is used for convenience, and this regulation can apply equally to turboprop-powered aircraft.) No change may be made in the takeoff configuration, other than undercarriage retraction. No power changes are permitted until the 400 ft height point is reached. FAR 25.111 (c) refers. FAR 25.111 further notes that the Takeoff Path may be continuous *or* by means of segments. (If continuous this will indicate a V_2 climb at Maximum takeoff thrust, or power, until any time limit for such a power level is reached.)

Flight Path Segments

The Takeoff Flight Path (*sic*) commences at a height of 35 ft above the takeoff surface at the end of the required TOD (TODR) – i.e. at the Screen height and point (FAR 25 115 (a)). (This point having been established as being the *greater of* the distance to the Screen, with one engine out from V_{EF} (as defined) *or* the distance to the Screen × 1.15 – i.e. 115% of the engine-out distance – but with all engines operating.) This may be, for the sake of comparison between the requirements of JAR 25, (G)JAR 25, and BCARs Section D, referred to as being Gross Flight Path. The Net Flight Path is the Gross Flight Path *reduced* by climb gradients equal to 0.8% for twins, 0.9% for tri-jets, and 1.0% for four-engined aircraft. Where the aircraft is accelerated in level flight these reductions also apply to the gross acceleration in such Acceleration Segment.

FAR 25.121 develops the one engine out concept. Let us now attempt to list, as far as is possible, the various segments and their associated requirements.

Plate 4 Clean aircraft from an unusual angle. (*Photograph courtesy of British Aerospace*)

1. First Segment
This is the element from V_{LOF} to the undercarriage fully-retracted point. The required gradient of climb must be Positive for twins, not less than 0.3% for tri-jets, and not less than 0.5% for four-engined aircraft, all as from V_{LOF}.

2. Second Segment
Also known as WAT, this is the segment flown with the undercarriage up and the Flaps at Takeoff setting. Like the First Segment, this must be carried out clear of ground effect. The required climb gradients are: not less than 2.4% for twins, 2.7% for tri-jets, and 3.0% for four-engined aircraft. The required speed is V_2.

3. Third Segment
Also known as Acceleration Segment, this is the first of the 'optional' segments. It may be used when obstacle clearance considerations permit the aircraft to level out and a horizontal attitude to be assumed, during which segment the aircraft is accelerated up to the Flap Retraction speed (V_{FR}), after which the aircraft is in the en route configuration – or, as it is more usually referred to, 'Clean'. Once the aircraft is 'cleaned-up' the climb is resumed at Final Takeoff Climb

speed (V_{FC}). The Third Segment may not be flown at a height of less than 400 ft above the takeoff surface.

Note
Any obstacle must be corrected for the effect of runway Slope. e.g. TODR = 1720 m, Slope = 0.5% Up, 0.5% of 1720 m = 27 ft. As the Slope is uphill the aircraft is increasing its height amsl, and therefore the obstacle in question is 27 ft less above the TOD point.

The Third Segment takes account of Altitude, Temperature (OAT), Speed (kt) and Wind Component (kt, Head or Tail). The resulting calculation gives horizontal distance from the levelling-out point (speed V_2) to the 'cleaned-up' point.

4. Final Takeoff Climb Segment
This comprises the segment existing from the chosen acceleration height up to an altitude of 1500 ft. The required gradients of climb for this segment are not less than 1.2% for twins, 1.5% for tri-jets, and 1.7% for four-engined aircraft, flown at a speed not less than 1.25 V_S.

Note
1. In considering the Net Flight Path and the gradients of climb required for the various segments it must be remembered that these segments give a *Gross* Flight Path. To obtain the *Net* Flight Path the results obtained thus must be *reduced* by 0.8% for twins, 0.9% for tri-jets, and 1.0% for four-engined aircraft.

2. Except, possibly, in the case of some of the earlier Flight Manuals the graphs presented in Flight Manuals may be read by entering with actual, or reported, values – e.g. OAT, Wind Component, etc. The resulting data extracted from each graph is *Net* and no diminishing or factoring is necessary. The *required* gradients of climb, or acceleration distances, are all included. Figure 5.1 shows a FAR 25 type Net Flight Path schematically.

JAR 25
JAR 25 follows FAR 25 for all essential purposes, as do the UK JARs. None of the *written* requirements contained in any of the foregoing Regulatory Requirements fully defines the profile of the Takeoff Flight Path, or Net Flight Path. No Segment numbers are cited, and neither is there guidance as to the number of segments involved. There is, however, general agreement as to the two initial Segments – i.e. the First Segment, which extends from the 35 ft Screen Height to the height at which the undercarriage is fully

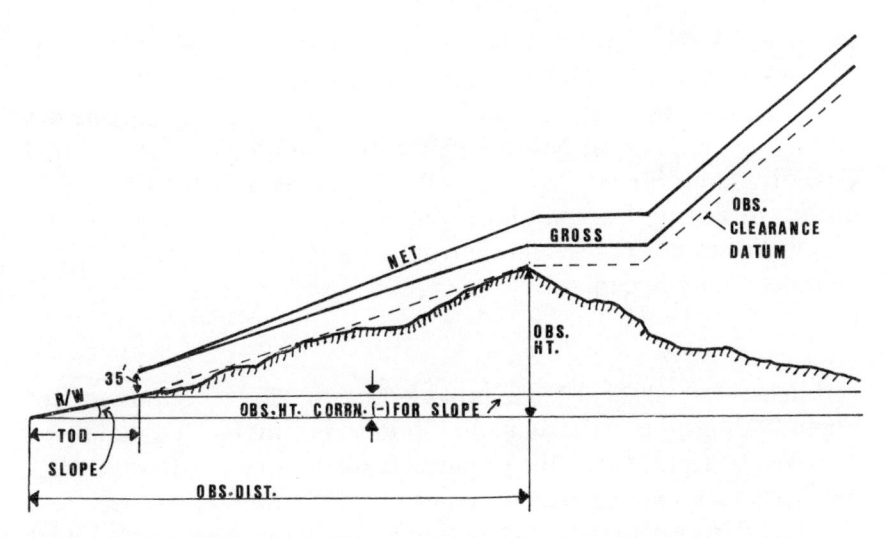

Fig. 5.1 Obstacle clearance requirements; the Gross and Net Flight Paths

retracted, and the Second Segment, with takeoff Flap still extended. This segment may extend up to any point at which any level flight acceleration element is introduced, with the lower level set at 400 ft, and the upper level up to the time-dictated point at which takeoff power *must* be reduced to Maximum Continuous Power, and the speed equals at least Final Takeoff Speed.

The whole concept of the Net Flight Path (which now only appears *named as such* in UK Requirements, such as BCARs Section D and the Air Navigation (General) Regulations) is, in fact, only specifically defined for the First and Second Segments. From the latter point a whole number of options are open. These range from the extended V_2 climb Second Segment up to the takeoff power cutoff altitude, as determined by a specified time limit appropriate to the engines, to a multi-segment profile. But, in the case of the BAe 146-100, the extended Second Segment based on a takeoff power time limit of 5 minutes from the opening-up to takeoff power, is not (currently) scheduled. Also available in the BAe 146-100 Flight Manual (JAR 25, as applicable to the UK) are up to five segments, including two level acceleration segments. Both of these level segments are available at the choice of the user, at altitudes that optimise any obstacle clearance requirements. (Remember, from Chapter 4, that a speed increment can be converted into an increased climb gradient, and this holds good following an acceleration segment). In the BAe 146-100 case, provision is made for a Third Segment during which the takeoff Flap setting is reduced to 18° (assuming that a higher setting is used for takeoff). The aircraft accelerates from V_2 to the Final Takeoff Climb Speed, after which the flaps are selected fully up. There follows a Fourth Segment during which the Flaps are retracting, and the aircraft is climbing at Maximum Continuous Power and at Final Takeoff Climb Speed (V_{FC}). A Fifth Segment may then be introduced, this being a second horizontal acceleration segment, during which the aircraft is accelerated from Final Takeoff Climb Speed to en route Climb Speed.

Note
1. Flight Manual Charts are provided to enable the optimum Net Flight Path profile to be calculated. It must be emphasised that these give *Net* data and that all the required gradients of climb for each segment are included, as are the required factors for converting Gross into Net Performance. In fact, it can be stated that all modern Flight Manuals give only Net data. The foregoing detail is provided solely to give the reader an idea as to the safeguards that are included in the Flight Manual data.

2. A word here about runway Slope and its effect upon the Net Flight Path. When checking the effect of an obstacle on a takeoff, and the requirement that it must be cleared by at least 35 ft, with one engine out, it must be borne in mind that the necessary obstacle clearance calculations are made beginning from the start of the takeoff, as regards distance. (This is because the 35 ft height point, or Screen height, is established from the TOD calculation, and therefore the screen position is identified. The 35 ft Screen height, in effect, marks the end of what is an initial segment, during which a height of 35 ft is achieved after a calculated distance.) Therefore the distance of the obstacle from the start of the takeoff is the basis of the calculation; imagine that a horizontal line is drawn from the takeoff start point, and a vertical line is dropped from the top of the obstacle. But it must not be forgotten that the Segmental Net Flight Path is initiated from a point 35 ft above Reference Zero (RZ). The RZ is simply the base of the imaginary Screen. (It may be defined as being a vertical line passing through the 35 ft height point intersected by a horizontal line drawn at the takeoff surface level.)

Now consider the runway Slope – i.e. the difference between the geographical elevations amsl at either end of the runway. Let us take, for example, a 2000 m runway and TODA, the start end of which is 500 ft amsl while the other, or Upwind end, is 520 ft amsl. We thus have an Uphill Slope – assuming that the whole of the TODA is used (i.e. 2000 m) the top of the 35 ft Screen will be, in fact, 55 ft above the start of the takeoff elevation (520–500) = 20+35+55 ft. If the vertical height of the obstacle is, say, 150 ft above the horizontal datum mentioned in the previous paragraph its *effective* height, relative to the flight path, is only 130 ft. In fact, due to the slope of the runway being upwards the aircraft taking off will have 'climbed' 20 ft by the time it reaches the 35 ft Screen, in addition to the airborne climb from V_{LOF}. Therefore it is 20 ft higher, relative to the obstacle, than would be the case were there no runway Slope.

An uphill Slope *reduces* the effective obstacle height, while a downhill Slope *increases* it, by the amount of the difference between the two runway threshold elevations. Or so the various operating rules being considered say.

Comment
This is not necessarily the case, and in fact is valid only when the runway Slope is constant. We have discussed the question of the Slope already in Chapter 1, as regards the takeoff up to the Screen height. It is appropriate that we should reiterate the fallacy inherent in the assumption (accepted by most regulatory bodies) that all runways are continuous plane surfaces as regards Slope. Applying this to the Net Flight Path ('Net' only being found in UK regulations), consider the case of a 'dished' runway (i.e. one where the surface elevation reduces between either end) having a length of 3000 m, by way of an example only. The elevation at the start end is 500 ft amsl and at the downwind end is 520 ft amsl. But, at the *required* 2000 m to the Screen (i.e. TODR) the elevation of the runway is only 460 ft. So, on takeoff, the aircraft crosses the Screen at a height of 495 ft amsl – i.e. 5 ft *below* the height amsl at which the takeoff was started, instead of 35 ft+the increment due to 0.2% uphill, namely 13 ft (20 ft rise in 3000 m is 0.2%, in round terms. 0.2% slope, over 2000 m, approximates to 13 ft). Now consider a constant slope 3000 m runway, having the same threshold elevations as in the previous case. This, too, will have a 0.2% Slope, which means that the elevation amsl at the Screen point is 513 ft, compared with 495 ft.

Ignoring the effect of the Slope on performance, for the sake of the example, (the TODR, in the 'dished' runway case would in fact be less than the 2000 m calculated for a 0.2% Uphill Slope, as the element to the Screen is Downhill) the elevation, amsl of the Screen base on the constant Slope runway will be 513 ft, and in the 'dished' case it will be 460 ft. Thus, at the Screen base, the height is 13 ft higher than the start elevation in the constant slope case, and 40 ft lower in the 'dished' case – i.e. a total difference of 53 ft. Yet, legally, both runways have a 0.2% Uphill Slope.

Assume now that there is an obstacle in the takeoff path having a height of 150 ft above the start elevation, and that this cannot be avoided by means of the maximum alteration of heading, in either direction, that is permitted. In the case of the constant slope runway, an aircraft taking off will have 'climbed' 13 ft+the 35 ft Screen height – i.e. 48 ft above the takeoff elevation. In the other case the aircraft will have dropped 40 ft amsl when it crosses the Screen, so that its height above the takeoff elevation 500 ft amsl will, in fact, not be above at all $(-40+35) = -5$ ft. In other words, it will be 5 ft below its takeoff elevation.

Thus, for the *approved* calculation, the constant slope case allows for the *effective* height of the obstacle to be $(150-30) = 137$ ft, for clearance. But, the same *calculation* legally is also applicable to the 'dished' runway case, as the Slope value is still considered to be 0.2% Uphill. But, in fact, the *effective* height of the obstacle to be cleared is not 137 ft, but 190 ft, the aircraft having 'dropped' 40 ft below its base (obstacle height at start being 150 ft above runway level, while the runway level at the Screen is 40 ft lower than at the takeoff start). So the relative differences between the *effective* obstacle heights are 53 ft – i.e. 137 ft in the constant slope case and 190 ft in the 'dished' runway case. Therefore, in the latter case an aircraft taking off will be that much lower in altitude, relative to the takeoff point, than the same aircraft taking off from the constant slope runway. This even exceeds the 35 ft required obstacle clearance – should the obstacle be critical and require the RTOW to be reduced, the aircraft in the latter case will be in a safe situation, whereas the other aircraft will be 53 ft lower. Yet, according to the approved calculation giving a 0.2% Uphill Slope for both, the conditions should be identical. However, the 'dished' runway aircraft should, by all the rules, have a point of impact with the obstacle some 18 ft below its summit! Admittedly an extreme and academic runway case has been used for the purposes of this illustration, and readers may take some comfort in the fact that it is highly doubtful that such a runway with such a profile would ever be built. But the principle is still valid, and is used for illustration purposes. (See Fig. 5.2.)

Both FAR 25, JAR 25 and (G)JAR 25, follow the foregoing in a similar fashion, in most respects anyway. However, while FAR 25 ends the Takeoff Flight Path at 1500 ft, JAR 25 and (G)JAR 25 have no specified upper limit. Instead, this is replaced by any altitude that is subject to the Takeoff Power time limit. (In the case of the BAe 146-100 this time limit is 5 minutes from the opening-up to takeoff power, and the altitude limit thus becomes the maximum altitude that can be attained, dictated by the need to achieve Final takeoff speed within this time, having regard for aircraft weight, ambient temperature, and so on. However, performance data for this climb procedure is not as yet, scheduled.)

Under these rules, therefore, the Flight Path may be any profile that complies with the individual requirements for each individual segment on the one hand, and the 5 minute limited Second Segment climb on the other. (This must not be interpreted to say that the

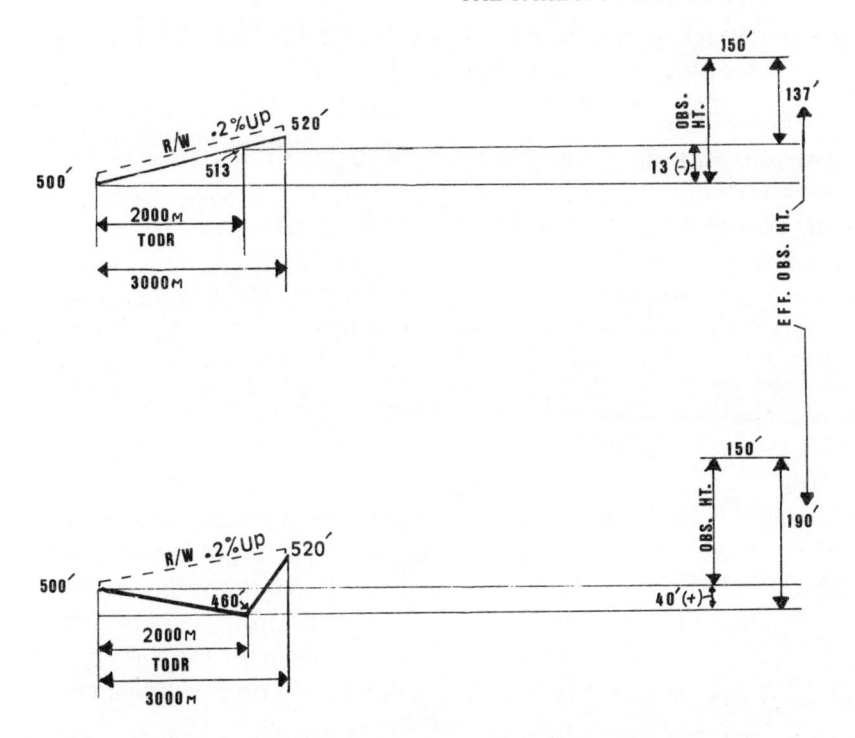

Fig. 5.2 Theoretical increase in obstacle height when runway is 'dished'

Second Segment may last for this time!) Therefore the exact method of scheduling the Flight Path data, by means of the Flight Manual (which forms part of the individual aircraft's Certificate of Airworthiness, by the way), is left to the aircraft manufacturer, and this must then be approved by the Regulatory Authority, subject to the Flight Path being confined within the regulatory envelope.

The BAe 146-100 Flight Manuals provide a single chart to cover 'near' obstacles – i.e. those up to 3750 m from the Screen position, or Reference Zero – and this chart combines the First and Second Segments. Where more distant obstacles are involved a separate *Second Segment only* chart is provided, together with charts for the Third Segment (Acceleration Segment), Fourth Segment (Climb with Flaps UP), and a Fifth Segment (Acceleration Segment). Also provided is a chart that enables a 'Reference gradient' to be established. This is an act of mercy, as it can be used to ascertain whether or not the Second Segment can enable all obstacles to be cleared up to the First acceleration segment altitude. If it does, there is no need to construct a Net Flight Path of multi-segments. Figure 5.3 shows a five segment Flight Path (Net); this is valid for (G)JAR 25. The actual conditions illustrated are as follows:

Takeoff Flaps	18°
Airport altitude	5000 ft
Ambient temperature (OAT)	+28°C
Reported Wind Component	20 kt Head
Runway Slope	1% Downhill
Reference gradient	4.3% (Minimum required = 3.0%)

(Editorial considerations preclude the inclusion of charts to illustrate this example.)

Turns

Data is also provided giving the radius of any Turn permitted (i.e. in excess of the 15° change in Heading allowed to either side of the takeoff direction) to clear obstacles in the Flight Path. This also provides horizontal distance covered during the turn. (In some Flight Manuals turn data is presented as 'Height Loss in Steady Turn'; there possibly may not be any height loss depending on the actual conditions. This is to cover any, quite normal, loss of climb gradient as a result of Bank during the turn.)

Incidentally, a Radius of Turn through up to 360° may be calculated by the following formula:

$$\text{Radius (feet)} = \frac{(V \times 1.69)^2}{G \times \text{Tan } \theta}$$

where V = True Air Speed (TAS) kt, θ = Bank angle, and G (Gravity) = 32.174.

Net Flight Path Profile

To sum up, the Net Flight Path can be constructed to almost any profile from the Flight Manual data, within the limits of that data, and this profile depends on the distance (m) and height (ft) from and above the Reference Zero point, or from the start of the takeoff point if TOD is added. (The RZ point is the base of the 35 ft Screen – i.e. the point on the runway (TOD) immediately below the 35 ft height point. Another difference between FAR 25 and JAR 25 is that FAR Flight Manuals often take the obstacle distance as measured from the start of the takeoff, by including TODR, while JAR 25 use the distance from the 35 ft height point. Both introduce the Gross to Net factor as from the 35 ft height point, though.) The FARs refer to a Takeoff Path, and also a Takeoff Flight Path; so do JARs. The

THE TAKEOFF FLIGHT PATH 69

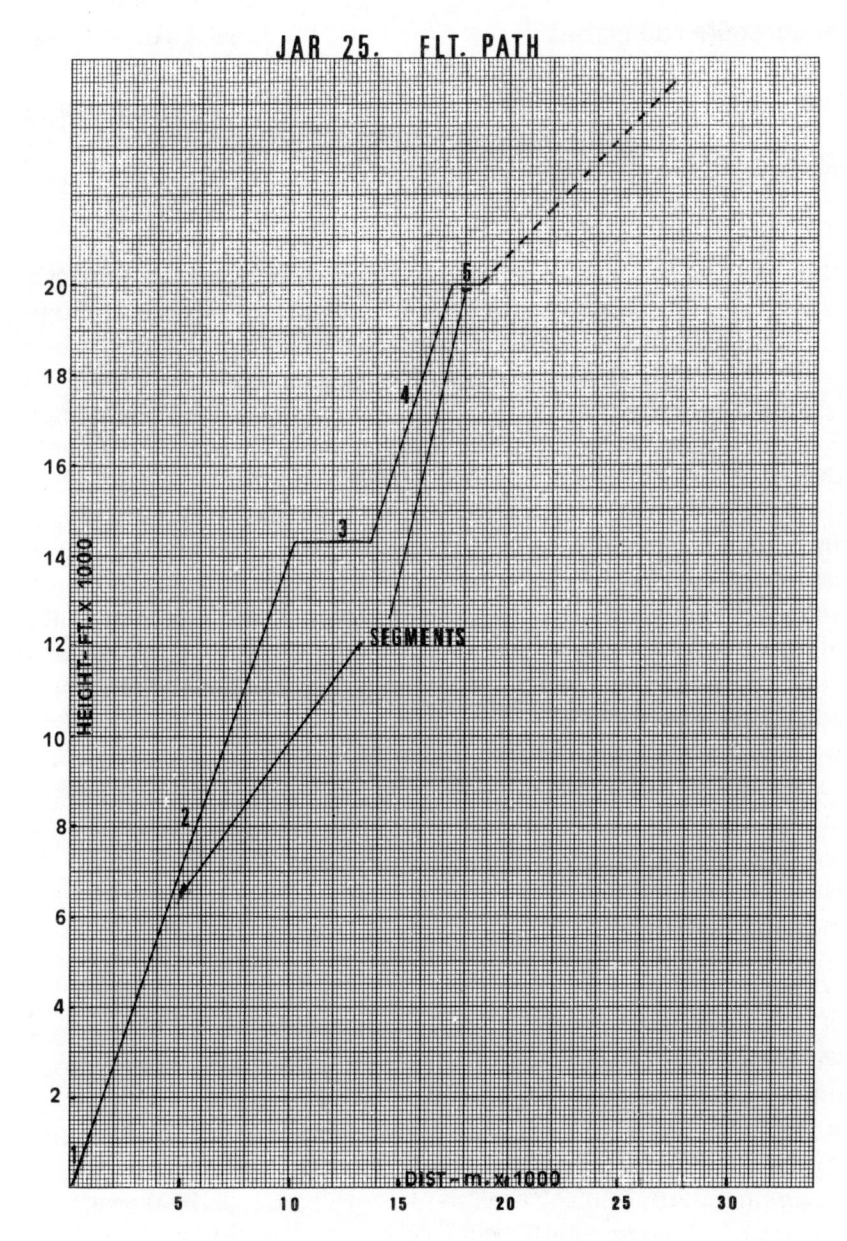

Fig. 5.3 Typical JAR 25 Flight Path profile

Takeoff Path extends from the start of the takeoff to a height of 1500 ft above the 'takeoff surface' (or runway, for simplicity's sake) (FAR 25.111 refers). The Takeoff Flight Path commences at the 35 ft height point; JARs follow suit. The FAR 25 Flight Path may end *either* at the 1500 ft height mentioned above *or* at the height at which the en route configuration is attained and the Final Takeoff steady gradient of climb is achieved (see FAR 25.111). The Takeoff Flight Path begins at the 35 ft point above the TODR (see FAR 25.113 (a) and FAR 25.115). But JAR 25 permits an 'extended' Second Segment, up to the takeoff power time limits, in addition.

Note
The First and Second Segments, it will be recalled, are the subject of WAT. This limitation is a function of Weight, for altitude and temperature, and is there to ensure that an acceptable post-takeoff climb gradient governed by these parameters can be attained. Thus WAT seeks solely to ensure an acceptable climb gradient for Weight in the First and Second Segments. However, when we are dealing with the Takeoff Flight Path, and specifically with the first two segments, we are, in fact, constructing a flight profile applicable to the RTOW, be this runway or WAT limited. As in the case of all Net Flight Path segments, the data for segments One and Two provide horizontal distance (m) for climb gradient (%), and herein lies the difference. But although WAT is part of the RTOW calculation, any weight obtained from the runway and WAT limits can be still further limited by obstacle clearance considerations arising *at any point* in the Flight Path (and, indeed, even en route, where mountainous terrain occurs). Sometimes it is necessary to make use of operational procedures, such as climbing above the airport to a pre-calculated height before setting course, due to either Flight Path or en route considerations. Turin, for example, used to require certain types of aircraft to use such a procedure.

BCARs
BCARs Section D specify the Net Flight Path segment by segment. The required gradients of climb agree with both FAR 25 and JAR 25, but Section D-4. 2.2(a) is qualified by 2.2(b) which deals with aircraft in the First Segment *not* having automatic Maximum Contingency Power selection. The required gross gradients of climb under this requirement are -1.0% (twins), -0.7% (tri-jets), and -0.5% (four-engined). (In other words 'rates of sink'!) The first two segments cover WAT requirements, including any limits on power before a height of 400 ft above the runway is attained. (An example could be Maximum Contingency Power.) The relative gradients above assume that manual contingency power is *available*.

At 400 ft above the runway there is an all-engines operating requirement, which states that at Maximum Takeoff Power the gross gradient of climb may not be less than 5%.

The Third Segment extends from 400 ft to 1500 ft above the takeoff surface and requires a minimum gradient of climb being not less than 1.2% (twins), 1.4% (tri-jets) and 1.5% (four-engined), this gradient being Gross. However, this segment may *either* be in the form of gross climb *or* its equivalent in horizontal acceleration.

The Final Takeoff Climb Segment is scheduled for both an engine out, and all-engines operating. In the engine-out situation, at a height above the takeoff surface of 1500 ft and in the en route configuration – i.e. cleaned up (whichever is the later), the required climb gradient may not be less than 1.2% (twins), 1.4% (tri-jets) and 1.5% (four-engined), in each case with the operating engine(s) at Intermediate Contingency Power. (Contingency Powers are specified for different engines in different aircraft types. They are not fully emergency power values, but offer a power value above Maximum Continuous when unexpected conditions indicate a need for more power.) After clean up, the speed may not be less than the greatest of:

1.1 V_{MCA} *or*
1.2 V_{MS1} *or*
1.08 the pre-stall buffet speed, at maximum continuous power.

The Final Takeoff Climb Segment also starts at the 1500 ft point, but in this case the minimum gradient of climb, gross, is 3%, at Maximum Continuous Power (MCP), and a speed which is 1.05 times the minimum of:

1.10 V_{MCA} *or*
1.20 V_{MS1} *or*
1.08 × pre-stall buffet speed in steady straight flight, with all engines at MCP.

The Final Takeoff Climb Segment is defined in BCARs Section D2-3 Appendix, 6.2, and D2-4 Appendix 2.7 and 2.8. Figure 5.4 shows the permitted Net Flight Path profiles.

Where 1500 ft height is reached before any time limit on Maximum Takeoff Power, the Net Flight Path may be based on flight with the Flaps at Takeoff setting, at the Maximum Contingency Power and Maximum Takeoff Power, as appropriate. In this case the horizontal acceleration segment (i.e. Third Segment) should be used to reach Flap Retraction Speed (V_{FR}), at the end of which process the speed for the aircraft in a cleaned up state, in the initial en route climb, must be attained. (BCARs D2-3. 6.3.2. (Appendix) refers.)

UK – Regulatory Sources
The UK not only has to pay due regard to the Airworthiness Requirements but also to the Statutory Instruments that are the force behind

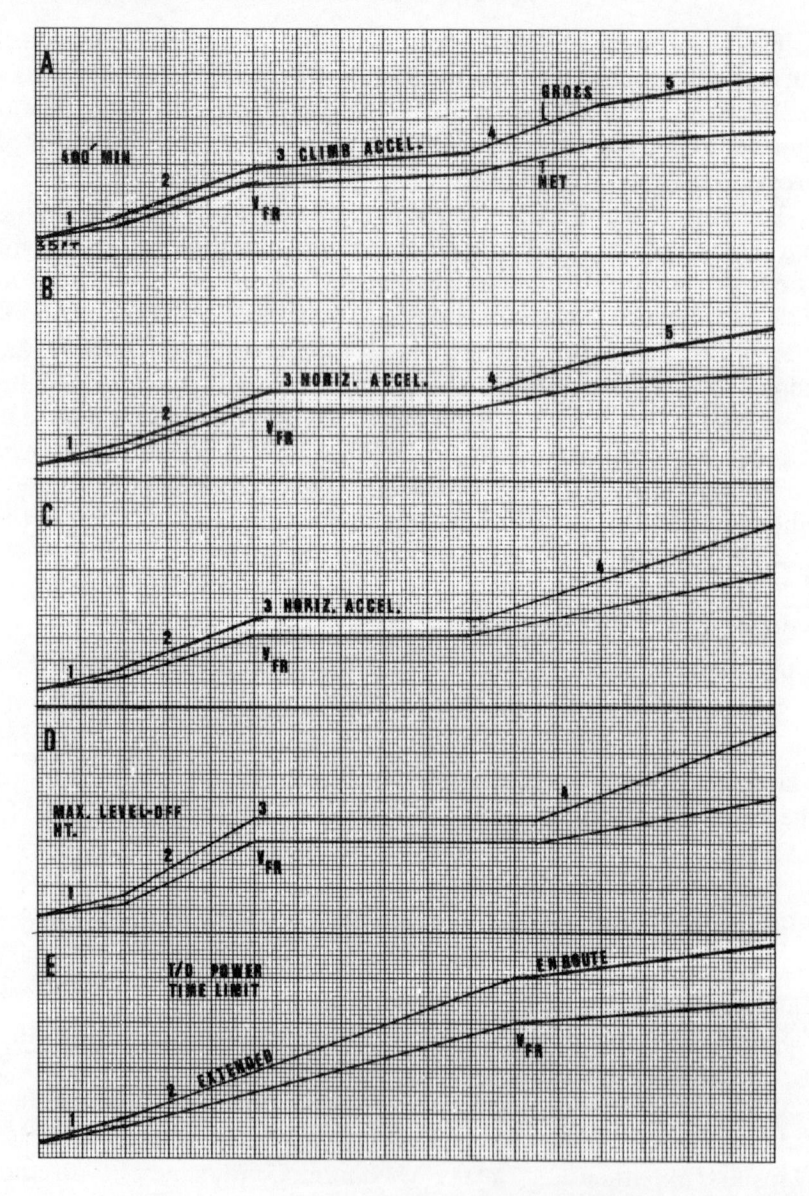

Fig. 5.4 BCARs Section D Net Flight Path profiles

these requirements. In particular, the Air Navigation (General) Regulations 1981 need to be borne in mind – in context of the Net Flight Path, Section 7 (3) (a) and (b) refer. These Regulations require that the Net Flight Path be plotted from the 35 ft height point, with one engine out, up to 1500 ft height above the 'aerodrome' (*sic*). Here we have one of the discrepancies that exist between the

Requirements and the Regulations – as regards the UK, at least. BCARs Section D requires that the later height be *at least* 1500 ft, whereas the Regulations (ANGRs) are specific – i.e. 1500 ft. During the Net Flight Path all obstacles must be cleared by 35 ft vertically, except where an aircraft makes a change in Heading *exceeding* 15°. Normally, for Performance considerations, any change in Heading during the Net Flight Path is due to obstacle clearance requirements. If the change in Heading exceeds 15° the required vertical clearance is increased to 50 ft during the Turn. This is an extra 'cushion' to compensate for any height loss during the Turn (ANGRs 7 (3) (a)).

An obstacle is deemed to be on the Track of an aircraft in the Net Flight Path if the distance from a point on the ground vertically below the aircraft does not exceed the following total distance:

60 m + ½ wing span + ⅛ of the distance from the point vertically below the aircraft from the TODA, *or* 900 m, whichever is the lesser.

In addition, the turn radius must not be less than that scheduled in the applicable Flight Manual for Radius of Steady Turn.

Comment on runway slope requirements and effects

Earlier in this chapter we considered runway Slope, and advanced a reason why this *could be* fallacious. An illustration was provided to support the argument advanced, this being of a hypothetical nature. The point behind the argument was that there could well be some cases in which the *calculated* height at an obstacle might be lower in practice, due to the effects of an assumed constant Uphill Slope. It must be clearly understood that the method of calculation used takes into account the one generally acceptable method of deriving the Slope of a runway – namely the change in elevation (amsl) between the ends of the TODA relative to its length. But, given the necessary data, it is the author's opinion that the somewhat vague Slope value can be made more accurate, and thus safer.

Reference has already been made in this book to certain instances where the Flight Manual contains data to enable the distance required to reach V_1 to be acquired. Most international airports have their operational characteristics published in detail in their National Aeronautical Information Publication (or AIP). In most cases charts giving the various runway profiles are also included, such charts being referred to as ICAO Type 'A' charts. These charts enable the Slope along the whole runway length to be ascertained, in the form of a number of elements, and the Slope then becomes available for each element, instead of the average Slope. So, with a 'dished' runway, and having the Slope applicable to various elements plus data giving distance required to V_1, it becomes possible to use a much more accurate method of assessing the overall effect of Slope on a takeoff. Firstly, we can locate the V_1 point more precisely, using the applicable Type 'A' chart Slope data and the Flight Manual performance data. Knowing the speed values required, by referring the 'accurate' V_1 to the TOD required and the value of V_2 it becomes possible to adjust the Screen position relative to this V_1, and a revised Slope can be estimated using the Type 'A' chart and TODR. Admittedly this is a somewhat complex calculation, but it will not normally be the pilot's job to carry it out. This is strictly an Operations Department's task! If a Type A chart is not available it could possibly be in an operators best interests to physically measure the profile of the runway using – say – a sextant to take runway slope readings at regular measured distances. (It is only necessary to construct a Net Flight Path up to the obstacle point. Once this is reached, and the required clearance is met, the calculation is ended – unless further, more distant, obstacles exist.)

Another, simpler, way to achieve the same end, although perhaps not to the same degree of accuracy, is in the case where the runway length available (TODA) exceeds that required (TODR). For example, there is a runway length available of 3000 m (TODA). The estimated TODR is 2000 m. Why use the Slope for 3000 m if it is possible to obtain a more accurate value, using the Type 'A' chart applicable to the first 2000 m of the runway?

6: En Route

We have now reached the point at which our aircraft has completed its takeoff and Net Flight Path. It is aerodynamically cleaned up – that is to say, that its Flaps and Undercarriage are fully retracted – and it has started its climb to the planned, or allotted, cruising altitude or Flight Level. We are not yet out of the regulatory wood, though, and various requirements have to be met that affect the En Route case. However, when compared to the Takeoff and Net Flight Path situations the En Route requirements are simple, and will need very little explanation. The requirements simply concern the gradients of climb with one or more power units inoperative en route.

General – FAR 25
Firstly, as usual, let us consider the requirements for FAR 25. FAR 25.123 decrees that data must be scheduled for the En Route configuration and situation. The most unfavourable Centre of Gravity (C of G) must be assumed, and cognisance must be taken of the instantaneous weight – i.e. the actual aircraft total weight *at the time* that the data is required to be applicable. In other words, at the time when the engine, or engines, actually fail. (This weight will be, for example, the actual takeoff weight minus the weight of the fuel burned, during the flight, up to the time of the engine failure.) The critical engine(s) will be inoperative, and the remaining engine(s) will be at Maximum Continuous Power (MCP). Temperature and Altitude must also be taken into account.

In the case of twins the actual gradient of climb with one engine out is *diminished* by 1.1% to provide Scheduled data. The appropriate value for tri-jets is 1.4%, while that for four-engined aircraft is 1.6% (FAR 25.123 (b)). The two-engines out case must also be Scheduled for both tri-jets and four-engined aircraft. The *available* gradient of the first category must be diminished by 0.3%, and for the second category by 0.5% (FAR 25.123 (c)).

JAR 25
JAR 25 also follows the same pattern and requires no further explanation. There are no national variants that concern us – e.g. (G)JAR 25.

BCARs

BCARs Section D2-4 specify that all-engines operating climb data must be Scheduled, gross (D2-4. 3.2). The one engine out data is Scheduled, being diminished by 1.1% for twins, 1.3% for tri-jets, and 1.4% for four-engined aircraft. It will be noted that, in the case of aircraft having more than two engines the requirements are less stringent than those contained in FAR 25.123 (b)).

In the case of the Scheduled climb gradients for aircraft having more than two engines and with two of these engines out, tri-jets are required to have the *gross* gradient of climb Scheduled, while the four-engined aircraft must have the gross gradient of climb, diminished by 0.3%, Scheduled as Net. To be strictly accurate, the Scheduling of two engines out climb data is discretionary. But if it is *not* Scheduled, Net, the aircraft may not be operated on any route where a suitable airport is, at any stage, more than 90 minutes flying time distant, using the two engines out prescribed power. In other words, the aircraft must at all times be within 90 minutes time of a suitable diversionary airport.

UK – Additional Requirements

The UK Air Navigation (General) Regulations amplify the foregoing requirements. Regulation 4 specifies that, with one engine out, and the remainder at MCP, the aircraft must be able to continue the flight, clearing all obstacles within 10 nm on either side of the required Track by at least 2000 ft, to an airport suitable for meeting the Landing requirements for an *Alternate* airport. (Chapter 7 deals with the Landing requirements.) The available gradient of climb, measured at a height of 1500 ft over this airport may not be less than 0%. (If suitable precision navaids – e.g. Very high frequency Omnidirectional Radio range (VOR) – are available the lateral obstacle requirement may be reduced to 5 nm on either side of the required Track.) The number of engines with which the aircraft is equipped is not specified and therefore Regulation 4 applies to twins, tri-jets, and four-engined aircraft equally, all having one engine inoperative.

Regulation 5 covers the two engines out case, but understandably it only applies to aircraft having three or more engines (no Regulatory body, to the best of the author's knowledge and belief, requires performance to be Scheduled covering total power failure, such as rate of glide with no power. Therefore, Regulation 4 allows for the twin, while Regulation 5 allows for the case of an aircraft having more than two engines, with two of these inoperative and *at least* one operating).

The two engines out requirement in Regulation 5(a) assumes that both engines fail – not necessarily together – at a distance greater than that which would be covered in 90 minutes flying time *at the all-engines economical speed* from the nearest airport that complies with the laid down requirements for Landing specified in the foregoing Regulation (Regulation 4). Likewise the En Route obstacle clearance requirements are the same.

Engine-out Conditions
Regulation 5(b) covers the case of a twin-engined aircraft with engine failure en route (subject to it *not* being limited to the carriage of *less than* 20 passengers, and having a Maximum all-up weight *exceeding* 5700 kg). In such a case the time from the nearest suitable airport that meets the requirements for an *Alternate* (see Chapter 7) may not exceed 60 minutes, at one engine out normal cruise speed. This regulation applies to aircraft such as the Boeing 737, F28, DC-9/MD80 etc.

As mentioned previously, engine-out gradient of climb data for the En Route case is Scheduled. This data has two applications. Firstly, it is used to establish the maximum altitude that may be attained, for the prevailing conditions of Weight, Altitude, and Temperature, following the failure of one or more engines after takeoff.

It might be thought, at first sight, that under these conditions the most prudent and sensible course of action would be to return to the airport of departure and then to land there. But this may not be possible, for reasons and requirements that have nothing to do with performance. For example, the takeoff may have taken place in meteorological conditions that were perfectly acceptable for a takeoff but which would be below the required limits (Aerodrome Operating Minima – AOM) for landing. In such a case the only acceptable course is to fly to the nearest suitable airport for Alternate compliance, at MCP, and then to land there. To do this the aircraft *must* be able to comply with the obstacle clearance requirements throughout the flight.

The second purpose of the engine-out cruise data is to cover the event of engine(s) failure at high cruise altitudes. In this eventuality the effect on the flight will depend on

Weight
Altitude
Temperature (OAT)
How many engines are still operating.

Drift Down

At high Flight Levels or Pressure Altitudes – i.e. indicated altitudes with the altimeters set to 1013.2 mb or 29.92 Hg – and depending on the aircraft's performance characteristics, a single engine failure *may* result in the aircraft being unable to maintain height. A double engine failure – especially in the case of a tri-jet – will almost certainly result in an inability to maintain high altitude (unless perhaps, the aircraft is very light) and the aircraft will slowly lose height. Eventually it will descend to an altitude at which it will be able to maintain height – i.e. the descent will be checked. This process is referred to as a Drift Down.

On all flights it is useful to know at what altitude the Drift Down ceases, and this is known as the Stabilising Altitude. With a single engine out, even in the case of a twin, the Stabilising Altitude will probably not result in any real problems, unless the Track passes over high, mountainous, terrain. The obstacle – or terrain – clearance requirements have already been given; if the Stabilising Altitude does not afford the required clearance (2000 ft) a serious problem arises. (The Fokker F28-3000 Performance Manual provides very comprehensive Drift Down data, including distance covered in the process from the engine failure point.)

When it is known that an aircraft's planned route, or Track, passes over high mountainous terrain the Stabilising Altitude must be established for the forecast meteorological conditions before the aircraft takes off. If the pre-calculated Stabilising Altitude provides the required obstacle clearance, with *any* engine failure point en route, no serious problems arise. If, however, the Stabilising Altitude works out at less than 2000 ft above the terrain on the route the engine failure point becomes significant. First, if this point comes before the critical terrain elevation, can the aircraft Drift Down so that it reaches its Stabilising Altitude +2000 ft clearance required *after* the critical terrain has been passed? (i.e. the aircraft passes over the obstacle, even though it is descending, *at least* 2000 ft above.) If not, then the route cannot be operated unless officially approved operational instructions to the pilot have been issued by the operator – e.g. the location of a Critical Point, where, subject to no engine failure having occurred beforehand, it is safe to continue the flight. If there are any doubts a high-terrain avoidance routing must be planned.

For the purpose of establishing the Stabilising Altitude point the worst case should be assumed. That is to say, the engine failure point must be assumed to occur so that the Zero rate of descent – and for that matter, climb – is reached over the highest terrain on Track, allowing for the option of either turning back before this point is reached, should engine failure occur, or continuing the flight with the required 2000 ft clearance. In whichever course is taken the aircraft *must* at all times be able to comply with the obstacle clearance requirements. In assessing the position, the weight of the aircraft is assumed to be its instantaneous weight at the time of (a) the engine-failure point and (b) the geographical position of the critical terrain elevation. (See Fig. 6.1.) In case (A), the pre-flight calculation has shown that the engine-out Stabilising Altitude will clear the critical obstacle by at least the required 2000 ft. Case (B) shows that the Stabilising Altitude is too low, while case (C) shows that the engine failure point, although close to the obstacle, results in an acceptable clearance.

Figure 6.2 gives the En Route Climb Gradient for the BAe 146-100, with one engine out. (A similar chart is used for the two engines

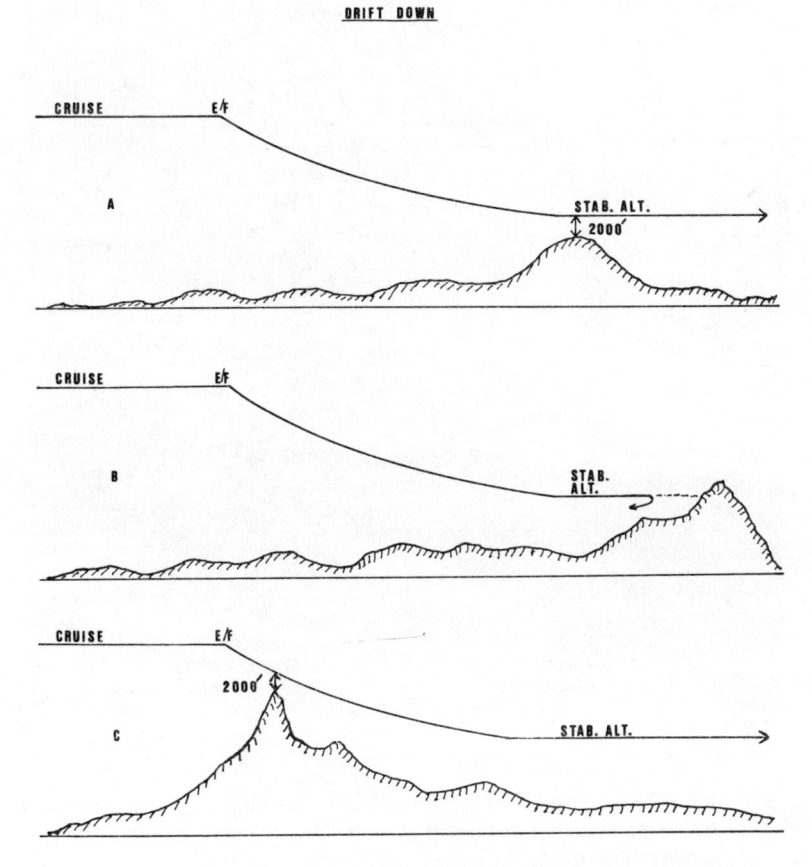

Fig. 6.1 Drift Down after engine failure en route; in A and C the flight may be continued on the intended Track, but in case B obstacle clearance cannot be achieved

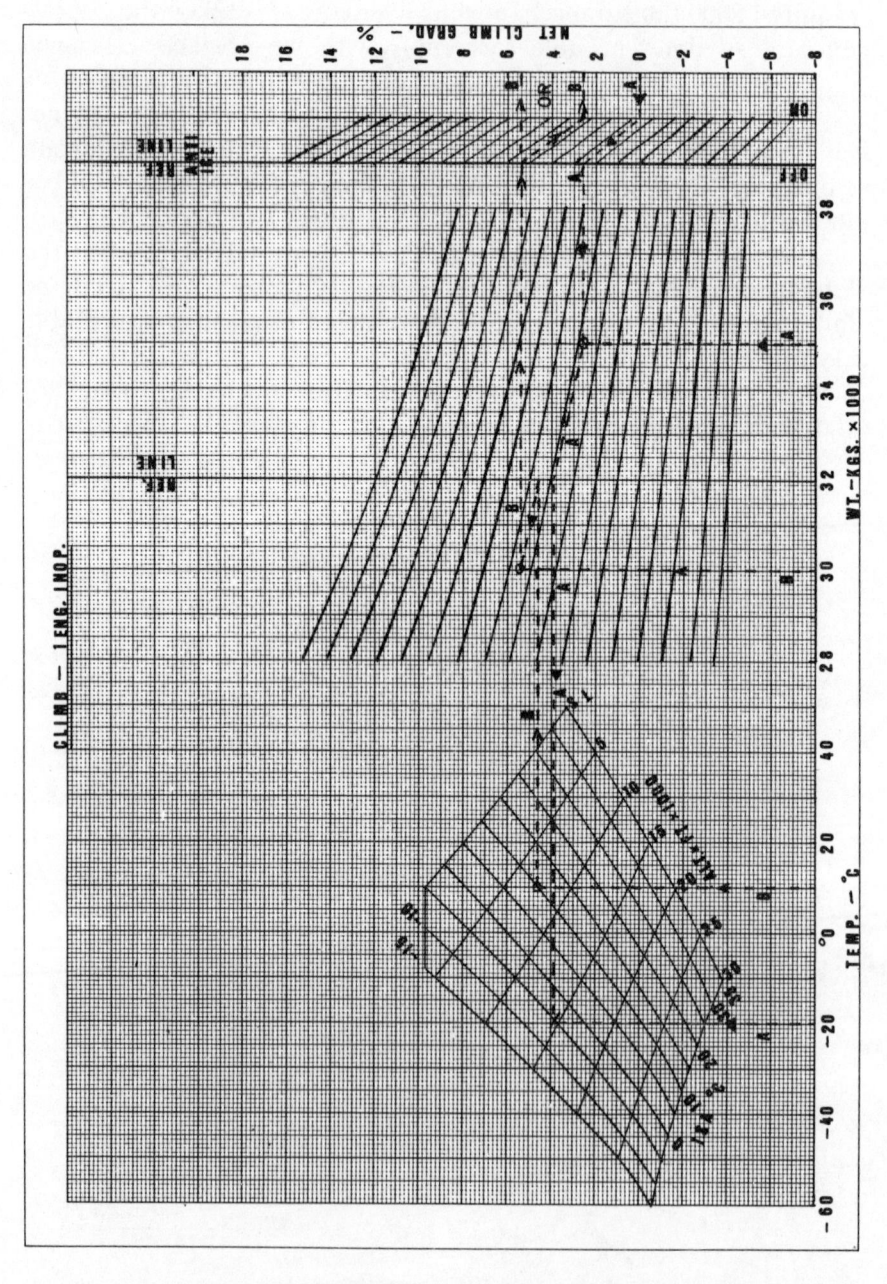

Fig. 6.2 The Net en route climb gradient. Stabilising Altitude is found by entering with 0 gradient and working back to the weight curve that is appropriate to temperature and altitude

out case; the effects of this extra power loss are noticeably more adverse.) This chart may be used in two ways. To ascertain the Net Climb gradient *available* the chart is entered from the left, with Temperature and Altitude. Proceed from the chosen altitude horizontally to the right, and the Weight section Reference Line. From the Reference Line follow the guidelines to the actual – i.e. Instantaneous Weight and then horizontally right to the engine Anti-icing On or Off grid. If icing conditions permit, the Off reading may be used – at least in practice, but the contingency of unforecast icing should be borne in mind at all times. It will be seen that the Net Climb gradient is reduced by some 2–3% with the Anti-icing bleed On, due to the resulting loss in available power. The foregoing process enables the Net Gradient of Climb, with an engine out, to be ascertained.

The other purpose of this chart is to enable the Stabilising Altitude to be established. To do this enter from the right of the chart at the 0% point, Anti-icing On, (preferably), and move horizontally to the left to intercept the Weight (actual) line projected vertically upwards. From this point follow the guidelines to the Reference line, and thence horizontally left to the Temperature/Altitude carpet. Project the Temperature line vertically upwards to intersect. Where the two lines intersect is the Stabilising Altitude.

Our example (A) in Fig. 6.2 takes the actual weight as being 35 000 kg, with Anti-icing On, OAT −20°C. It will be seen that the Stabilising Altitude for these conditions is 14 800 ft. Still using the same chart it is now required to find the Net Climb Gradient available, with one engine inoperative, for a given set of conditions. These are: OAT +10°C, Altitude 7500 ft, Weight 30 000 kg, Anti-icing On. (Example (B).) Enter the Temperature/Altitude carpet with +10°C and move up vertically to intercept the Altitude 7500 ft. Now move horizontally right to the Reference Line, then follow the guidelines, left, to intercept the vertical Weight line for the actual weight 30 000 kg. From this intersection point move horizontally to the Anti-icing Reference Line and follow the guidelines down to the On vertical. Move right to the Gradient scale and read off the Net En Route Climb Gradient 2.6%. The engine-out climb gradient is calculated using the en route climb speed applicable to the Instantaneous Weight.

Stall Speed at High Altitudes
One final point concerning the en route situation is the effect of altitude on the Stall speed, Equivalent Air Speed (EAS), and IAS. The EAS has been taken from the Indicated Air Speed and then corrected for compressibility and for Air Speed Indicator (ASI) Static position error. IAS is only corrected for instrument error. Stalling Speed (V_S) is a function of EAS, physically.

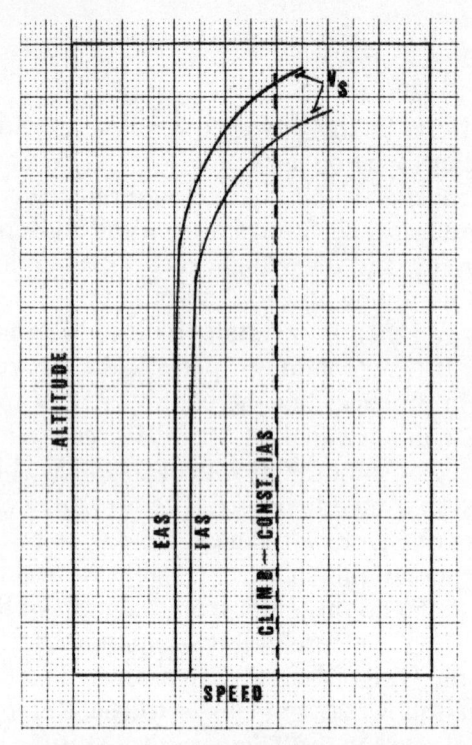

Fig. 6.3 How V_S increases at high altitudes

However, in considering V_S and the climb, one must remember that the relationship between EAS and IAS remains fairly close and constant for much of the climb. When the higher altitudes are reached, both values increase in the context of V_S, and this increase is not equal. The higher the altitude the less the rate of increase for V_S in EAS than for IAS. Thus, if the climb is maintained for a constant value of EAS, and at a high climb gradient, the climb speed EAS will first reach the V_S in IAS, and then in EAS. Therefore it can be very hazardous to 'struggle for height', in search of fuel economy, and will probably not necessarily work in these terms either. While the Fuel Flow may reduce so might the True Air Speed (TAS), and the net result could be reduced nautical air miles per kg of fuel. Also, the aircraft may well stall, into the bargain. At high altitudes not only should the levelling out to cruise altitude be carried out in good time, but it should be carried out well above the stall speed. (See Fig. 6.3.) This question is largely academic, as no aircraft manufacturer who values its name would provide information relating to conditions outside safe operational parameters. But the fact remains that, at the top of a climb to high cruise altitudes, V_S increases significantly in terms of both EAS and IAS, and the margin between the climb IAS, EAS, and V_S becomes less and less with altitude. Some pilots have had to learn this the hard way. The moral is – never try to cruise at any altitude above that recommended in the aircraft's Cruise Control data – which is not certificated, by the way.

7: Descent and Landing

The Landing is the concluding phase of a flight, and the Landing Distance Required is scheduled. However, unlike the other flight elements there is no temperature accountability – only altitude. The landing performance is based on the landing being carried out in International Standard Atmosphere (ISA) as appropriate to the airport's elevation. Account must be taken of Slope and Wind Component and the Landing Distance Required differs according to whether the runway is at the intended Destination or the designated Alternate. In the latter case the requirements are less stringent.

We have, in the course of this book, covered the Takeoff, Climb-out, Climb, and Cruise requirements. These are all subject to certification and to being scheduled in the aircraft's Flight Manual; this document forms part of the aircraft's Certificate of Airworthiness, it will be recalled. It therefore seems strange that the Descent is *not* Scheduled, although the actual Landing is. So, in the course of each flight, from the start of the takeoff to the end of the landing roll, there is one element that is not covered in the Scheduled Performance, namely the Descent. Although to be fair this is a fairly simple and straightforward procedure.

Descent
The actual Descent is normally the flight element commencing at the Cruise altitude (or Flight Level) and ending at an altitude of 1500 ft above the airport of destination. There are two main considerations that affect the performance aspects, namely Descent Speed expressed in IAS or in Mach No. values, and the Cabin Rate of Descent. The performance information is normally presented in a Flight Planning or Cruise Control Manual. Although outside the Flight Manual it can be taken for granted that the data is accurate and safe as it has almost certainly been checked by the regulatory authorities.

The first consideration is one of safety, and involves structural considerations. In the hands of an idiot there is nothing to prevent an aircraft being *dived*, rather than descended, with the object of building up a high speed and rapid descent. This could have dangerous repercussions as a result of structural limitations – in fact, the wings might well suffer from structural failure if the speed is allowed to build up to something more than that for which the structure was designed to tolerate. In the 'Limitations' section of the Flight Manual will be found two speed values that *must* be observed at all times. These are Maximum *Normal* Operating Speed or Mach No., and Never Exceed Speed or Mach No. (V_{NO}/M_{NO} and V_{NE}/M_{NE}). There is also a V_{MO}/M_{MO} value to be considered; this is Maximum Operating Speed or Mach No.

In practice, the rules for compliance with these Limiting Speeds are simple to understand and are, in themselves, almost self-explanatory. V_{NO}/M_{NO} *may* be exceeded if operationally necessary, but otherwise is the maximum speed available for normal operations. V_{MO}/M_{NO} should not be exceeded other than in the case of an extreme emergency, and then only for the minimum time possible, while V_{NE}/M_{NE} is what it says – *never* to be exceeded, otherwise structural damage may occur. The Descent speeds provided by the aircraft manufacturer infringe none of these Scheduled Limiting Speeds, but normally appear as a range of speeds that permit the selection of a steep descent at one end to a shallow descent at the other. For example, the F28-3000 allows for descents ranging from 320 kt IAS/M.725 down to 230 kt/M.6. The first is a High Speed Descent, the latter for Long Range.

Cabin Descent Rate and Flight Profile

The other factor affecting the Descent is Cabin Pressure. Normally this should not exceed 500 fpm, and the stated pressure differentials in the manufacturer's data should not be exceeded. Thus, the aerodynamic, and structural, rates of descent that may be acceptable can be subject to the rate of descent of the cabin, and this must not be excessive. Too high a cabin rate of descent can produce at best, discomfort, and at worst, serious injury or even death to the occupants. Again, if the manufacturer's performance data is adhered to, no problems should arise during the Descent. The whole flight profile can affect the Descent, and this depends on the operator's requirements and economics. On short haul routes a trajectory-type profile may have benefits, for example, while on others a long, slow, Climb to cruising Flight Level (FL), at the completion of which a slow, shallow, Descent may be preferable. The former procedure may involve a short time only at cruise level, with a steep climb and descent. The latter often involves a long, shallow, climb, followed by a high level cruise (or possibly, on a long flight, two or more cruise Flight Levels), climbing to new FLs as weight decreases, or OAT permits, and then a long, shallow descent. Usually the main consideration, whether for economic or operational reasons, is the amount of fuel that is used during the whole flight. It is difficult to be precise as to which is best, for a number of reasons. At the time of writing, fuel is the most costly item of all the flight costs items. At the same time the total flight costs, excluding fuel, but based on time, may indicate that a minimum time flight is in the best interests of the operator. The characteristics of different aircraft types, too, play their part. For a steep climb, for example, an aircraft may burn less fuel than it would on a shallow climb. But it would also probably cover less distance, so that the nampkg (nautical air miles per kg) for the climb could exceed a shallower climb's value. Likewise, the cruise distance would also be increased, but the fuel flow for the cruise would be significantly lower. The shallow descent will probably give (a) the better distance-for-time and (b) the lower fuel burn. In effect, it becomes an extension of the cruise, with a small reduction in speed but a large reduction in fuel flow.

One of the most critical aircraft, as regards sensitivity to the effects of weight, OAT, and altitude when considering the climb, cruise, and descent, was the Bristol Britannia 310 series. The climb, and initial cruise, would largely be dictated by all three values, after which it became very sensitive to OAT and its effect on Cruise FL. It was quite normal to have to reduce FL due to OAT after a few hours of flight, only to then need to climb up again, hopefully to an even higher FL than the first, as dictated by the gradient of climb availability at the time, due to the OAT variations. Normally this varying flight profile only applied to the longer routes, where nampkg was the primary consideration when a long-range requirement ruled overall.

Landing WAT
When dealing with the Landing, it will be found that the first item that must be considered, and calculated, is WAT, just as we had to in the takeoff case. Here we must ascertain the gradients of Climb for both the Approach, and the Landing configurations. The requirements will be gone into later in this chapter, but the purpose of this scheduled – i.e. Flight Manual – data is to ensure that the aircraft can climb away throughout the Approach and airborne part of the Landing. Also scheduled is the Missed Approach case, and the runway distance required; the latter is the distance to come to a complete stop from a height of 30 ft (BCARs), *or* 50 ft (FARs) *or* both (JAR 25, Method 1 or 2), having regard to the runway Slope, the Wind Component, airport Altitude, and the All-up Weight of the aircraft. There is *no* temperature accountability; all landings are assumed to take place in the International Standard Atmosphere (15°C at sea level, reducing by approximately 1°C per 500 ft increase in altitude).

Landing – FAR 25

Let us now consider the Landing phase in detail, as we did for the other Scheduled elements of a flight. Once more we will start with FAR 25, and then examine the requirements and differences contained in JAR 25, (G)JAR 25, and BCARs Section D.

FAR 25.119 requires that the available steady gradient of Climb, in the Landing configuration, may not be less than 3.2%. The available power, at the takeoff position of the throttles – i.e. the takeoff power available for the conditions – must be attained within 8 seconds of the selection of takeoff power. In other words, the engines must be able to 'spool-up' from the power being used for the Landing to the power available for the OAT and altitude within a maximum time of 8 seconds (FAR 25.119 (a)). The climb speed associated with the prescribed Climb gradient above must be not *more* than $1.3V_S$. (This will give a steep climb with a safe margin over V_S.)

FAR 25.121 (d) specifies the requirements for the Approach configuration, in which the all-engines operating stalling speed V_S may not exceed 110% of V_S appropriate to the Landing configuration. The available Climb gradients, under these conditions may not be less than 2.1% for twins, 2.4% for tri-jets, and 2.7% for four-engined aircraft, all with the critical engine out and the remaining engines at Maximum *available* takeoff power, at Maximum Landing Weight (MLW) and a climb speed not exceeding $1.5V_S$.

The gross Landing Distance is specified as being the distance required to cross a 50 ft screen and come to a complete stop, in International Standard Atmosphere (ISA), at the altitude of the airport surface, and at the appropriate weight, this not exceeding MLW. Account must also be taken of the Wind Component, and this must be factored as in the takeoff and climb-out cases, restricting the permissible assumption of the Head wind component to be only 50% while the Tail wind component must be increased by the *addition* of 50% – i.e. the familiar 50%/150% rule.

The aircraft must be:

1. In the Landing configuration.
2. A 'gliding' approach must be assumed at a CAS (Calibrated Air Speed) of not less than $1.3V_S$ down to the 50 ft height point.
3. Changes may be made in the configuration, and to the power and speed in order that the landing procedure conforms with normal practices.
4. Somewhat quaintly, or perhaps unnecessarily, the landing must be made without, it is decreed, sudden drops, bouncing, nosing-over, or ground looping. Such things, and their avoidance, are ever in the mind of all pilots! (Besides which, the passengers do not like it.)
5. The Landing must be made without the need for exceptional skill on the part of the pilot.

Thus FAR 25.125 (a).

FAR 25.125 (b) continues in a similar tone:

1. The use of the brakes must be as specified by the manufacturer thereof and any limitations must not be exceeded.
2. The use of the brakes must be such as to avoid excessive wear in the case of either the brakes and the tyres.
3. *All means of retardation* that are available may be used – e.g. spoilers, lift dumpers, *reverse thrust,* etc. as long as these means are reliable and safe, consistent in effect, and do not affect the control of the aircraft adversely.

The permissibility for the use of reverse thrust is somewhat strange, because, to the best of the author's knowledge and belief, no FAR 25 Flight Manual has ever been issued that allows credit to be taken for this means of retardation. It is felt that this inconsistency can be traced to FAR 25.125 (b)(3)(i) which requires that all retardation devices for which *credit* may be taken must be safe and reliable. It can only be assumed that the FAA has not yet been satisfied as to the latter requirement, as reverse thrust may be *used*, and almost invariably is, during Landing. But, the Landing Distance requirement (LDR), as specified in FAR 25.125 (a) is subject to a large factor when compared to that called for under other regulatory bodies. In fact, the LDR must be factored by 1.67, and all landing data charts in FAA Flight Manuals contain this increment. This factor applies to the Destination airport. For the Alternate the factor is 1.43. (FAR 121.195 and 197.)

The Wind Component for landing is subject to the familiar 50%/150% factor. And FAR 25.125 (f) specifies that, if any device is used that relies on the operation of *any* engine, and if the landing distance is increased noticeably when landing with that engine out, then the Landing Distance required must be scheduled assuming that engine to be inoperative. However, if the engine failure can be compensated for by other means, the resulting landing distance must not exceed that for all-engines operating.

It may have struck readers that the factoring, or additions to, the Required Landing Distance have moved from FAR 25 to a different part of the Federal Aviation Regulations, i.e. Part 121. In fact, the whole matter has been made the subject of the *operating* regulations, rather than those relating to Airworthiness, or Performance. It will be useful, it is felt, if the relevant Part 121 provisions are examined in detail.

Landing Distance Factoring

FAR 121.195 deals with the regulations covering *Destination* airports. To meet the requirements the distances, or runway length

Plate 5 A Fokker F28 with all aerodynamic means of retardation extended. No thrust reversers are fitted. (*Photograph courtesy of Fokker BV*)

requirements, are factored as mentioned above, depending on whether the airport is the Destination or Alternate. Apart from the fact that the temperature is ISA, and not OAT, for the altitude, the runway assumed must be (a) the most favourable, *in still air* and (b) the most suitable in the forecast wind velocity for the Expected Time of Arrival (ETA). A special proviso is made regarding turboprop aircraft, these not (frequently) having means for reversing, although they can be made to increase Drag by the use of Ground Fine Pitch – i.e. disc-ing the propeller blades. Such aircraft may plan to use the airport with the conditions as in (a) above, even if it cannot meet the requirements for (b). It must, however, have an Alternate declared that enables it to land within 70% of the LDA, should the forecast conditions not be met for the Destination.

Specifically affecting jet aircraft only, FAR 121.195 (d) requires accountability for Wet, or slippery, runways. In such conditions, whether actual or forecast, the LDA must be at least 115% of that actually required. Also, should the conditions for the Destination, as defined in (a) and (b) in the preceding paragraph, not be met *at the time of takeoff,* the flight may still proceed if the necessary Destination requirements are met at the declared Alternate. (FAR 121.195 (e).)

DESCENT AND LANDING

To summarise this somewhat involved regulatory matter, any turbine-powered (jet or 'prop) aircraft must have at least 1.67 of the required Landing Distance to be available at the Destination, either in still air for the optimum runway or in the forecast wind conditions for a secondary runway. So, there must be at least two runways available to cater for the effects of wind – e.g. the case of a single runway with a limiting crosswind, or a tailwind component on a uni-directional runway, would not meet the requirements. A turboprop may *plan* and depart for an unsuitable Destination, if made so by wind conditions as long as it can land legally at a nominated Alternate within 70% (1.43) of the LDA. A jet aircraft must be able to land at a Wet Destination subject to the LDA being at least 115% of the LDR, and it may *plan* and depart for an unsuitable Destination (due to wind conditions), subject to an Alternate being available that meets all requirements for a Destination.

The requirements for an Alternate airport are compatible with FAR 121.195 (b) but the available length of the LDA must not be less than 1.43 times that required in the case of jets and 1.67 for turboprops. (FAR 121.197 refers.) In all cases, the Landing Distance Required (LDR) is measured from a Screen height of 50 ft to the point at which the aircraft comes to a complete halt after landing.

JAR 25

So much for FARs; we now turn to JAR 25. In particular let us look at JAR 25.125. JAR 25.125 (a) shows us that there are two methods available and open to the aircraft manufacturer, for the certification of landing performance. The first of these is identical to FAR 25.125, as augmented by the operational requirements of FAR 121.195 and 197. There is, therefore, no need for any further explanation touching on this method. In the second method the difference is considerable, and needs some explanation.

JAR 25.125 (b) establishes the Reference Landing Distance requirement in ISA temperature variation relative to altitude and weight, on a Hard, Wet, surface. The Screen height, though, is 30 ft, unlike the 50 ft in FARs. A 5% (i.e. 3°) Glide Path is assumed. The Speed associated with this procedure is initially the Maximum Threshold Speed (V_{Tmax}), measured at the 30 ft height point. V_{Tmax} is defined as being:

All-engines operating – V_{AT_0} + 15 kt, and
One engine out – V_{AT_1} + 10 kt.

V_{AT_0} is the Target Threshold Speed (TTS), all-engines, while V_{AT_1} is the TTS with one engine out. Touchdown must be made at the Reference Touchdown Speed, which is associated with the TTS V_{AT_0}; it must be not less than the normal touchdown speed and at least 5 kt *less than* the Maximum Measured Touchdown Speed. This latter is the highest all-engines speed at which contact may be made with the runway and *maintained*.

The Approach configuration must remain constant down to the 30 ft height after which normal configuration and power changes may be made – e.g. Spoilers may be extended and reverse thrust may be applied, after power reduction. *Under JARs credit may be taken for reverse thrust.*

Plate 6 A BAe 146 with all aerodynamic means of retardation deployed. No thrust reversers are fitted. (*Photograph courtesy of British Aerospace*)

The fundamental difference between the First (FAR type) and Second methods for scheduling the Landing Distance Required so far, relates to the procedure. The first method assumes a speed reduction to the minimum compatible with safety, at the threshold. This *can* result in some heavy landings, as the speed margin is not adequate to ensure a clean touchdown if the speed is misjudged. It is an effective way, though, of establishing the shortest landing distance. The second method is made at a faster speed, and this provides a greater margin for variations in handling and for errors. A faster

Plate 7 BAe 146 on approach. (*Photograph courtesy of British Aerospace*)

touchdown, followed by prompt use of all means of retardation, results in a cleaner landing.

The Approach and Landing Climb requirements are contained in JAR 25.119 and 121 (d). The former contains the requirements for the all-engines operating case. These state that, in the Landing configuration, the steady climb gradient must not be *less than* 3.2%, with the engines at the thrust, or power, that can be attained after moving the throttles from Minimum Flight Idle to takeoff power, within 8 secs. The required speeds are:

1. (a) A climb speed *not less than* $1.15V_S$ for aircraft with four engines which have a significant reduction in V_S as a result of power application
   (b) $1.2V_S$ for all other aircraft.
2. A speed *not less than* V_{MC_L}
3. Not more than *the greater of* $1.3V_S$ and V_{MC_L}.

JAR 25.121 (d) gives the Discontinued Approach requirements. These state that, for a configuration where V_S is *not greater than* 110% of V_S for the related all-engines landing configuration, the steady climb gradient must *not be less than* 2.1% for twins, 2.4% for tri-jets, and 2.7% for four-engined aircraft. The associated conditions are:

1. Critical engine out, and the remainder at the available takeoff power or thrust

92   HANDBOOK OF AIRCRAFT PERFORMANCE

2. Maximum Landing Weight
3. A normal established speed for landing, *not less than* 1.5V_S
4. Undercarriage UP.

We now turn to the scheduling of the Landing Distances Required, which must be the greater of the *All-engines and one-engine out cases*.

First, the *All-engines* case. This is the Reference Landing Distance, already referred to, multiplied by the *greater* of 1.24−0.1 C_{DG}:C_{DA} or 1.11. The *one engine out* case is the *greater* of 1.19−C_{DG}:C_{DA} or 1.08.

The Ratio C_{DG}:C_{DA}, in simple terms, is the ratio of Effective Groundborne to Airborne Drag.

The Landing Distance *Required* for the Destination is multiplied by 0.95 to obtain the Required Landing Distance for an Alternate. Figure 7.1 refers; it gives the landing performance (LD) Required for the BAe 146-100.

Comment
A small question seems to pose itself here. Are we comparing like with like? For example, the Required Landing Distance at sea level can be substantially less than that required at, say, 5500 ft. Thus the required LD at the Alternate *could* be greater than the required LD at the Destination if the Alternate is at a high altitude − e.g. Destination: Mombasa, Alternate: Nairobi.

Reference has been made to a few speed values relating to the scheduling of landing performance under JAR 25. It is felt that a more complete, and fuller definition, of all Landing and Approach Speeds would be of value; these are listed below, together with the appropriate JAR 25 references.

Approach and Landing Speeds − JAR 25
APPROACH AND TOUCHDOWN SPEEDS
1. *Target Threshold Speed (TTS)*−V_{AT}
   All-engines, V_{AT_0}
   V_{AT} may not be less than *any* of the following:
   (a) *either* V_{S_1}+22 kt, where V_{S_1} is appropriate to the Approach configuration *or* 1.3×V_{S_0} (Stall speed for the configuration, with all-engines operating) *whichever is the lesser*.
   (b) V_{MC_L} (Minimum Control Speed for Landing);
       Minimum Demonstrated Threshold Speed+5 kt (see below);
       A speed 10 kt less than the final steady approach speed, all-engines;

DESCENT AND LANDING 93

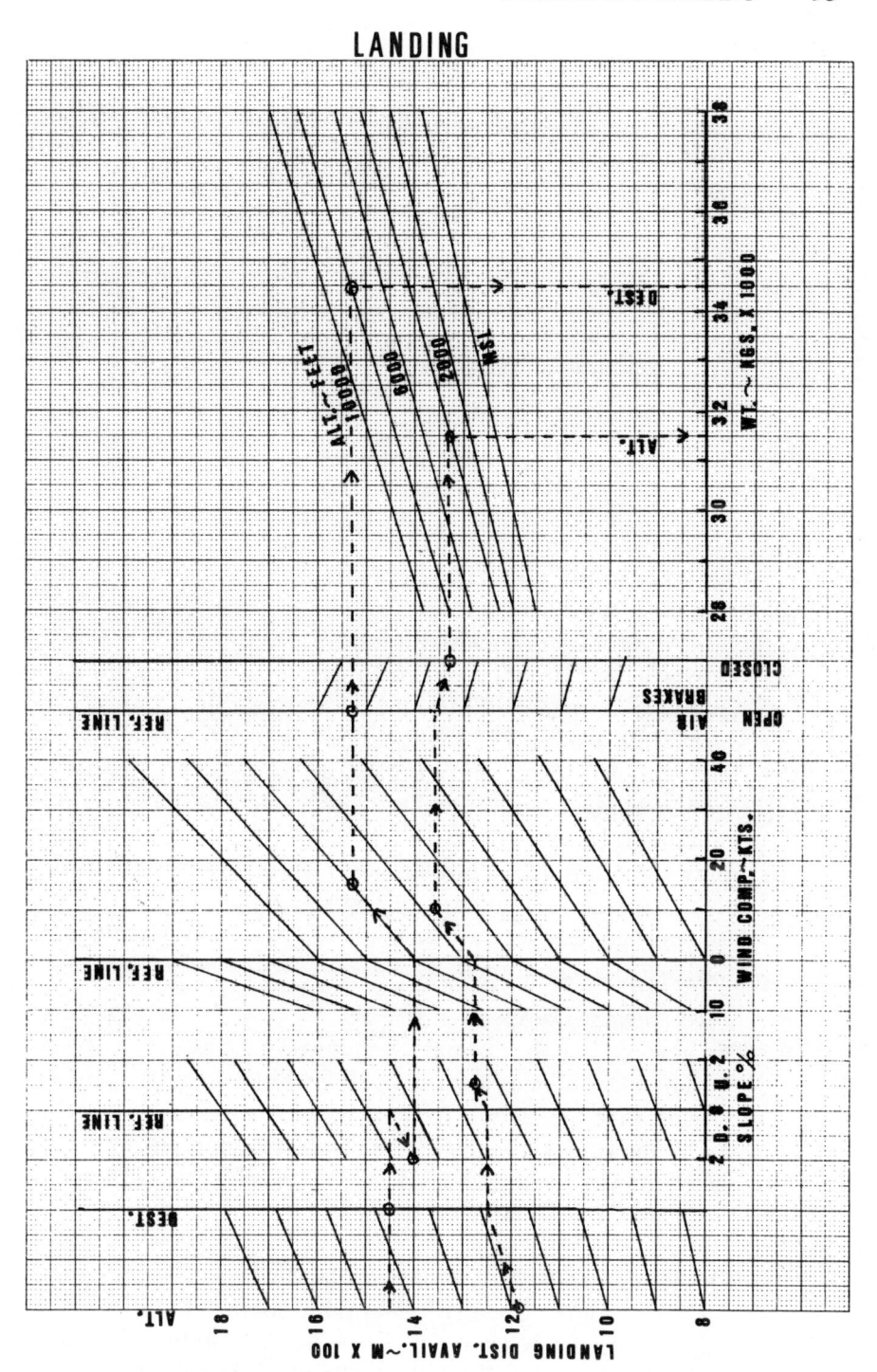

Fig. 7.1 Derivation of Regulated Landing Weight for Landing Distance Available, at Destination and Alternate

1.08×the speed for the onset of pre-stall buffet, in steady, straight, flight on a 3° Glide Path (G/P), in the Landing configuration.

One engine out, V_{AT_1}

V_{AT_1} may not be less than *any* of the following:
(a) V_{AT_0};
(b) $V_{MC_{L-1}}+5$ kt;
(c) In the case of aircraft with three or more engines a speed sufficient to complete the landing in the event of the second critical engine failing on the approach;
(d) A speed 10 kt less than the final steady approach speed.

2. *Maximum Threshold Speed* – V_{Tmax}
   (a) $V_{Tmax} = V_{AT_0}+15$ kt, all-engines
   (b) $V_{Tmax} = V_{AT_1}+10$ kt, one engine out.

3. *Minimum Demonstrated Threshold Speed*
   The lowest speed at the 30 ft height point, in calm conditions, from which the Approach, touchdown, and landing may be completed in the following conditions without hazard:
   (a) From a height of 200 ft down to the 30 ft height point the Approach is made at Minimum Demonstrated Threshold Speed, with a stabilised gradient not less than 5% (= 3°);
   (b) Zero rate of descent before touchdown;
   (c) Configuration down to the 30 ft height point normal for that point and landing;
   (d) Below the 200 ft height point no changes in power, other than those necessary to maintain an accurate Approach;
   (e) Only normal changes may be made to power and/or configuration *below* a height of 30 ft.

4. *Reference Touchdown Speed*
   A speed not less than the normal touchdown speed associated with V_{AT_0}, or any higher speed for use in high wind conditions, and at least 5 kt less than the highest speed at which contact may be maintained with the runway. (This allows for the effect of gusting, and possible Wind shear effects.) JAR 25.125 (c) refers to all of these Approach and Touchdown Speeds.

JAR25X135 requires accountability for landing on a slippery runway – i.e. a runway having a very low braking coefficient of friction. At the time of writing this accountability is detailed in the form of a recommendation only, contained in ACJ 25X135, and allows for the following procedures or values:

(a) Braking coefficient 0.05
(b) Reducing reverse thrust, down to 50% of full reverse thrust
(c) A higher Screen Speed, *not exceeding 10 kt*

The UK Variants to JAR 25 in context are small, and are contained in (G)JAR 25.121 (d)(3) and (G)JAR 25.125 (a)(10). The former covers the Discontinued Approach and requires the normal JAR 25.121 (d)(3) procedure and a speed *not exceeding* 1.5V_S, but with the additional requirement that the horizontal distance required to accelerate to this speed at the Decision Height must not exceed 10 000 ft.

The latter requirement decrees that the Target Threshold Speed must be derived in the manner appropriate to JAR 25.125, as summarised in (1) above. The Approach speed must be maintained down to a height of 50 ft, and must be *not less than* V_{AT_0} *or* $V_{AT_1}-5$ kt, whichever is the greater.

Thus it will be seen that the UK Variant only modifies the Landing Performance as laid down in JAR 25.125 (a). This is the FAA 25.125-type schedule, or JAR 25.125 'Method 1'. The whole emphasis of the UK regulatory requirements is to place the approach and landing emphasis on the value of a higher speed margin over the Stall speed for the configuration, thus accepting a higher touchdown speed with its concomitant slight increase in risk *solely due to the higher speed,* but asserting that this extra slight risk is more than offset by the resulting increase in landing accuracy. Thus lower factors can be accepted for the required landing distance than those for the FAR schedule. Depending on the aircraft type, of course, the resulting scheduled landing distances, including the factors, are probably not all that far apart.

BCARs
JAR 25.125 (b), or 'Method 2' is very similar to the BCARs rational landing concept. Having dealt with JAR Landing requirements let us now take a look at the now superseded BCAR D2 and the requirements therein for Landing. Sub-section D2-4 covers Climb, and we can conveniently start by taking first of all the Landing WAT requirements. Probably the first item contained in D2-4.4, in the Landing WAT requirements is the integration of landing weather requirements. Let us summarise the Landing WAT requirements:

1. For Decision Heights *not less than 200 ft*:
With all engines operating, at MCP and in the final approach configuration, the gross gradient of climb, at the runway surface and at the steady approach speed, must be *positive*. (D2-4.2.)

The Discontinued Approach case is covered in D2-4.4. At the runway altitude the gross gradient of climb must be *not less than* 1.1% for twins, 1.3% for tri-jets, and 1.4% for four-engined aircraft, all with the critical engine out and the remaining engines at Maximum Continuous Power. The required configuration is *either* the configuration for one engine out (D2-8. 3,4 refers) *or* the configuration that can be attained within 10 seconds of the start of the one engine out approach procedure. The appropriate speed is not less than $1.2 V_{MS_1}$ *or* for four-engined aircraft, where V_S is significantly reduced by the application of power, $1.15 V_{MS_1}$ as appropriate to the configuration for a one engine out Discontinued Approach procedure.

The Baulked Landing case, at runway level, requires a gross gradient of climb of not less than 3.2%, with all-engines operating at Maximum takeoff power and at a power *available* 8 seconds after initiation of a Baulked Landing, with the configuration appropriate to Landing, or subject to certain other conditions which we can conveniently leave out for our purposes (D2-8,,5.5.2 refers) the configuration that can be attained 5 seconds after starting the Baulked Landing procedure. The associated speeds are not less than $1.2 V_{MS_1}$, or $V_{MS_1} \times 1.15$ in any configuration in which the use of power results in a significant increase in V_S (this latter applies to four-engined aircraft only). The speed may not be less than V_{MC_L}, with one engine out, and not greater than V_{AT_0}.

2. For Decision Heights *less than 200 ft*:

The all-engines requirement is the same as in (1) above. With one engine out, at the altitude of the runway and with the aircraft in the critical engine out approach configuration and with all remaining engines at Maximum Intermediate Contingency power, the gross gradient of descent must not be *greater than* 2.0% for twins, 1.8% for tri-jets, and 1.6% for four-engined aircraft. (D2-4.3.)

Discontinued Approach and Baulked Landing

The Discontinued Approach, with the critical engine out, requires a gross gradient of climb of 1.1% for twins, 1.3% for tri-jets, and 1.4% for four-engined aircraft, with all remaining engines at Maximum Contingency power. The configuration must be *either* that appropriate to the one engine out approach, *or* that which can be attained within 10 seconds after the start of the one engine out procedure. The required speeds are not less than $1.2 V_{MS_1}$ *or* for four-engined aircraft where the application of power results in a significant reduction in V_S, $1.15 V_{MS_1}$, in the configuration appropriate to a one engine out Discontinued Approach procedure. (D2-8, 3.7 refers.) See also D2-4.4.

DESCENT AND LANDING

The speeds may also be *not less than* $V_{MC_L}+5$ kt and *not greater than* the final steady approach speed with one engine out, as specified for the aircraft type.

The Discontinued Approach for aircraft certificated to use a Decision Height of less than 200 ft must have a gross gradient of climb not less than 2.5% in the following conditions:

(a) Critical engine out, remainder at Maximum Contingency power;
(b) *Either* the final approach configuration for all engines operating as for the conditions in D2-8, 3.4, *or* in the configuration that can be achieved within 1200 m horizontally from the start of the procedure for a Discontinued Approach, with engine failure late in the approach;
(c) A speed not less than $1.2V_{MS_1}$, or for four-engined aircraft where the application of power results in a significant reduction in V_s, $1.15 V_{MS_1}$ where this latter value is appropriate to the configuration as specified for the aircraft type for a one engine out Discontinued Approach procedure. The speed must also be *not less than* V_{MC_L} for the configuration as in (b) above +5 kt. The speed should also be *not greater than* the recommended Decision Height speed. (D2-4.5 refers.)

The Baulked Landing requirement specifies that, at the runway altitude, the gross gradient of climb must be *not less than* 3.2% in the following conditions:

(i) All engines at Maximum takeoff power and at a power *not greater than* that available 8 seconds after starting the Baulked Landing procedure with the engines and thrust-reversers (or reverse pitch, for turbo-props) in the most adverse setting that can be obtained during the approach and airborne element of the landing;
(ii) The landing configuration, *or* such other approved configuration that may be attained 5 seconds after the start of the Baulked Landing procedure;
(iii) A speed *not less than* $1.2V_{MS_1}$ or for four-engined aircraft where the application of power results in a significant reduction in V_S, $1.15V_{MS_1}$ where V_{MS_1} is appropriate to the selected configuration for the procedure (D2-8, 3.7). The speed must also be *not less than* V_{MC_L} as appropriate to the configuration for a one engine out landing, *nor must it be greater than* V_{AT_0}.

3. Where approaches are carried out with an engine out intentionally – e.g. training flights, Type-ratings, etc.

All the requirements contained in (2) above apply. In addition, at the runway altitude the gross gradient of climb must not be less than 3%, and the engines must be operating at Maximum Contingency power.

Let us now turn our attention to the Landing runway requirements. These are contained in BCARs Chapter D2-5, and are similar to those for JAR 25.125 (b) 'Method 2'; an alternative method is also provided for that echoes FAR 25.125. A look at BCARs D2-5, 7 is as good a way as any to start, as we are provided with a definition. D2-5, 7.1 defines the Reference Landing Distance as being the distance needed to land, and come to a stop, from a height of 30 ft. This distance is then corrected to include the effects of a Reference Wet Hard Surface. The speed at the 30 ft height point is V_{Tmax}, and the Reference touchdown speed, like V_{Tmax}, is the same as for JAR 25.125 (b). These requirements were covered earlier in this chapter. D2-5, 7.2 specifies that the configuration for landing shall be constant down to the 30 ft height point, after which any other changes in the configuration that are normal and established may be made. For example Spoilers, Lift Dumpers, etc. may be selected after the 30 ft height point has been reached. All means of retardation may be used, and credit may be taken for their use, provided that these means are used correctly and the controllability of the aircraft is not adversely affected. Due allowance must be made for any malfunction of retarding devices; for example, if the required landing distance is dependent on the use of reverse thrust (or power) this distance will clearly be adversely affected if an engine is inoperative. This contingency is taken care of by requiring that the Landing Distance be scheduled on the basis of taking the *greater of* the all-engines and one engine out landing distances after applying the appropriate factors. These are the same as for JAR 25.125 (b), namely 1.11, *or* 1.24−0.1CDg/CDa, *whichever is the greater,* for all-engines, and 1.08, *or* 1.19−0.1CDg/CDa, *whichever is the greater* for one engine out.

The foregoing landing distance requirements are those applicable to the Destination airport. As with JAR 25.125 (b) the Landing Distance required for an Alternate airport shall be the Destination required distance×0.95.

BCARs D2-5 also provides for a 'FAR-Type' scheduling of landing distance, but with one notable difference. D2-5, 6.4.1 specifically *excludes* the measurement of landing distances using reverse thrust. This method of scheduling is referred to as being the Arbitrary Landing Distance; it is applicable to the older aircraft in service where subject to BCARs. The assumed Screen height is 50 ft, and the Glide Slope is 3° (5% gradient). The approach speed to the screen is *the greater of:*

$1.3V_{MS}$ *or* V_{AT_0} *or* V_{AT_1}−5 kt.

8: Additional Performance Considerations

This chapter is intended to discuss certain performance considerations where some elements of inaccuracy have to be accepted and tolerated. In the main, these areas of imprecision average out in relation to each other. But there is no firm reason why they should not all, on occasion, gang up together and produce a noticeably adverse, or even favourable, discrepancy as regards the *actual* runway distance or overall performance level that is achieved. For example, the takeoff weight for a given runway that is limiting will normally be calculated assuming the distance available from threshold to threshold. But what happens to the distance that is used in the process of turning on to the runway and lining-up? This could well be a significant percentage in terms of the distance available.

In previous chapters the author has made use of 'Comment' paragraphs that, in his view (and also, that of others, in certain cases at least) show that the various requirements cited have 'grey', or even blank, areas. These are where the requirements fail to cover the element of risk, either wholly (that is to say, as wholly as may be expected) or in part. And, to be fair, at least one regulatory authority is aware of deficiencies and is concerned over the situation, while another such body has taken the first, if tentative, steps to try and deal with the same area of concern.

Aborted Takeoffs
The main area of concern is the takeoff, and more specifically the aborted, or rejected, takeoff. From 1970 to the early 1980s (up to early 1984 at least) there have been a number of fatal accidents recorded that, in theory, should not have happened. The main ones that are performance-related and, in particular, affect the takeoff all involve either improperly executed aborted takeoffs or takeoffs that were continued but which should have been aborted.

As has been mentioned earlier, the takeoff performance is scheduled on the basis that an engine will fail during the takeoff, *and this is the only clear risk-element that is specifically allowed for.* (Probably because it is the only one that can be allowed for.) When – or where – this engine fails, determines the required action that must be taken to contain the risk acceptably. We have seen so far that, for each and every takeoff, there exists a decision point, with which is associated a Decision Speed. Should an engine fail, and such failure be *recognised* before or at the Decision Speed – V_1 – all the regulatory authorities mentioned in this book require that the takeoff *must* be aborted. There are no options, except in the finely balanced case of V_{EF} with recognition at *exactly* V_1. Only at this speed is the pilot allowed to choose his line of action from two alternatives.

To fully understand this point it must be considered further, with its other mandatory requirement, namely the continued takeoff. Under all the rules being considered and discussed, should an engine fail, with recognition occurring *at* or *after* the Decision Speed, the takeoff *must* be continued. But again the same 'point of choice' remains – the takeoff may be aborted *at*, but not later than, V_1.

Comment

Does it not seem illogical that such a highly significant speed, such as is the case with V_1, should be subject to such a crude means of identification? In reality, of course, V_1 is but one-half of a required ratio, the other half being distance. V_1 in isolation means precisely nothing; it *must* be associated with distance rolled for it to be meaningful. And to rely solely on an air speed indication is both crude and inadequate. And this has, sadly, been proved to be the case, on too many occasions and with the loss of too many lives. Airliners these days can both fly, navigate, and land themselves, without a human hand touching any controls, other than to occasionally press a computer button. The only exception is during the takeoff and initial climb period. To identify the vital Decision Point, a simple instrument that has changed little during the last 70 years is used – the ASI. And this only gives half of the vital ratio mentioned above.

In Appendix B and Appendix C to this book two fatal accidents, in which the V_1 concept was proved to be totally lacking in real meaning, are analysed. These two accidents are chosen as 'samples', because they bracket a period of some 12 years. Both are the subject of an official accident investigation and Report, and embrace the period 1970–1982. There were other accidents of a not dissimilar nature during this period; the two mentioned are simply useful illustrations at the beginning and end of the period mentioned.

The scheduling of the V_1 concept is, of course, better than nothing. But, it is maintained, for V_1 to have any *real* meaning the attainment of this speed *must* be related to the distance actually rolled in attaining it. Even more to the point, V_{EF} must be related to a distance point, and therefore to a required minimum acceleration level. It is not only the speed at which the engine fails; it is also *where* it fails that is vitally important. The problem, officially, is (a) how to determine the amount of runway being consumed, accurately and continuously, and (b) how to integrate this with the air speed being attained, also continuously.

ADDITIONAL PERFORMANCE CONSIDERATIONS

In broad terms, during the flight test programme of an aircraft type, the speed:distance relationship is measured very frequently, involving a large number of takeoffs under widely differing conditions. From these measurements, after processing, a fleet-mean level of speed:distance is obtained. This means that, with acceptable deviation limits, it is assumed with a high degree of justification that for any given value of IAS a certain amount of runway distance will have been consumed. The various safety factors are then added and only then is the takeoff performance data supporting the V_1 concept actually scheduled.

As is shown in the Appendices, a takeoff accident can occur during what appears to be a perfectly normal takeoff without any engine failure at all. There have been too many instances of this and the authorities are concerned – and rightly so. In the considered opinion of the author, and others, neither of the accidents analysed in the Appendices need have happened, and nor need many others. But before discussing this further we must take a close look at other matters that affect the takeoff and to which reference has already been made in previous chapters.

Some Ambiguities Affecting Takeoffs

The takeoff is not simply a matter of achieving accurately a specified level of speed:distance relationship. It has already been emphasised how crude is the basis upon which this relationship is scheduled. In fact, in actual everyday operations, permitted practices can be crude in the extreme, in the author's opinion. The scheduled takeoff performance, as presented in the Flight Manual, is based on a number of variables. These are:

(a) *ambient* Temperature
(b) *pressure* Altitude
(c) *estimated* Weight
(d) *average* runway Slope
(e) *reported* Wind.

In fact one, some, or all, of these variables may be significantly inaccurate, apart from Temperature. At least this value is accurately measured, and is not normally subject to sudden significant change.

Pressure Altitude, is the first source of potential error. Current, and officially accepted practice, is for the airport's geographical altitude to be used for calculating takeoff performance. But the scheduled performance is normally given for Pressure Altitude – i.e. the altitude represented by an atmospheric pressure of 1013.2 mb (29.92 in Hg). Density Altitude is Pressure Altitude corrected for temperature. But, it must be asked, how often is the actual air pressure 1013.2 mb? It could easily be, say, 990 mb or 1030 mb. Set an altimeter to the geographical altitude – i.e. the altitude of the airport – and the sub-scale will then indicate the actual air pressure – the value of which is available, and is normally provided by the airport authorities anyway.

Because of the difficulties associated with the provision of operating data that is subject to so many variables it has become common practice to use geographical altitude, or elevation, as a basis for calculation of the takeoff data. This calculation is fairly long-winded and is not, therefore, made by the flight crew but by the operator's operations staff. This will almost certainly entail the use of geographical elevation amsl and here is the first source of potential error – or even probable error – namely, the deviation between the elevation that will be used and the *ambient* pressure. In an ideal world the pre-calculated takeoff data would have provision for entering the data with the ambient, atmospheric, altitude, as indicated when the altimeter is set to the airport's *reported* pressure.

Fortunately, altitude variations are not *very* significant on their own, or in isolation. So let us move on and take the next variable, (c) or Weight. While the Operating Weight Empty (OWE) of the aircraft is accurately known, it having been physically weighed, the next significant weight is the APS Weight (Aircraft Prepared for Service Weight). This is the OWE, plus the *estimated* weight of the total crew, crew baggage, navigational equipment, passenger service items (e.g. toilet fluids), catering, and perhaps certain operating fluids not included in the OWE, such as Water Methanol (if used). Last comes the Required Takeoff Weight, and this is the APS Weight, plus the Sector Fuel and the Payload. But, in the case of passenger flights at least the weight of the Payload is *estimated* by using Standard Weights for passengers. Males are deemed to weigh 75 kg (if over 12 years of age), Females are said to weigh 65 kg, children under 12 but over three years old are deemed to weigh 40 kg, and infants under three, 10 kg. Passenger baggage is also deemed to have a standard weight, per piece, and this weight varies according to whether the flight is Domestic, European, or Intercontinental, and also whether or not it is scheduled or a holiday flight. Within these limits each piece of baggage may be deemed to weigh between 10 kg and 16 kg, according to the type of flight. Cabin baggage weighs 3 kg. (UK Air Navigation (General) Regulations, January 1988 refers.) On certain transatlantic flights, baggage may be treated volumetrically for the purposes of estimating weight, as well as to determine the free allowance. Thus the whole idea of estimated weights for passengers and baggages derives from the use of averages.

Consider an aircraft with, say, a load of 300 passengers. At least, pre-takeoff it will be known how many males, females, children, and infants will form this number, and therefore a *standard* payload weight can be estimated. But, let us suppose for argument's sake that these 300 people are all males. Ergo, the total weight of the passengers is 300×75 = 22 500 kg, according to 'The Book'. Fair enough – but now consider that the flight is, say, a charter carrying 300 males from either an ethnic group, or a profession in which males are traditionally large – e.g. dockers or policemen. What then? It is not unreasonable to assume an individual weight, under these circumstances, of 90 kg per person, so that the total will weigh 300×90 = 27 000 kg. But the weight will, in fact, still be deemed to be only 22 500 kg – an error of 4500 kg, or 20%, on the adverse side in the Payload alone. This error, as a proportion of the total All-up Weight, may not be serious, and certainly does not happen often. But, as regards Weight, there is again room for error.

Next in order, for the provision of possible inaccuracies – in order sequentially, that is – we find Slope (d). This we have already gone into in some detail as being a potential breeding ground for serious inaccuracies, but the context was that of the Net Flight Path (Chapter 5). Let us remind ourselves that runway Slope is currently calculated by the difference between either end of a runway in terms of elevation above msl. This is also an officially permitted practice. If the runway thresholds are at the same geographical altitude then there is officially, no Slope, and no correction need be made for this variable. (Figure 5.2 gives an illustration that is worth referring to now.) But should this runway have a pronounced 'hump', this could result in a significant Uphill Slope for the first part of the takeoff, and this would displace the V_1 point adversely, away from the start of the takeoff. In the case of an aborted takeoff from, or near to, V_1, the deceleration Slope would be mostly (and significantly) Downhill. Consider, for example, a runway 2500 m long, and with both thresholds at, say, 800 ft each above msl. At the mid-point of the runway, though, the elevation is 850 ft. 2500 m equals 2500×3.2808 = 8202 ft. The Slope is, therefore (assuming, for convenience, that the 'hump' is at the runway mid-point) 100/4101×50 = 1.21% (4101 ft at the mid-point). This Slope will be 1.21% Uphill for the acceleration element to V_1 and the same value, but Downhill, for the Deceleration element. Assuming, again, that the runway is limiting – i.e. that an aircraft is taking off at the maximum weight permitted by the available runway length, and *assuming zero Slope*, as is permitted, what then is the true position as regards the effect of this Slope?

Firstly, the assumed example envisages that the aircraft will be taking off on a level runway, and this is *not* the case. Secondly, the takeoff calculation will have produced a takeoff weight (RTOW) that allows for V_{EF} and V_1 at around the middle of the runway. But this point will *not* be at the assumed position at all. Because the acceleration will be essentially Uphill up to V_1, this highly significant point will be far closer to the other end of the runway than has been allowed for. Consequentially there is less distance available for aborting from V_1 than has been assumed to be the case. But, thirdly, any deceleration element for such an aborted takeoff will not only be less than supposed, but it will *not* have a level surface. It will, in fact, have a Downhill Slope of 1.21%. Just to put some numbers to this hypothetical, but not at all impossible, case – in the case of the BAe 146-100, 1900 m ASD becomes 1830 m effectively, with 1.21% Downhill Slope. In fact, nearly 4% less.

Slope Profile
Among the few aircraft manufacturers that recognise the importance of Slope *profiles* are Fokker BV of Amsterdam. In both the F27 and F28 Flight Manuals, data is provided whereby the ASDA can be broken into two elements, namely that which applies to the distance to V_1 and secondly that which applies to the distance from V_1, in the aborted takeoff case. This enables the ASD calculation to be made far more accurately. In our assumed 'humped' runway case the ASD required can be calculated by finding the distance *to* V_1 using the first half of the takeoff runway's Slope, and then finding the distance required to stop from V_1 using the second half. (See Fig. 8.1.) Means for establishing a runway's actual Slope profile were discussed in Chapter 5. The 'humped' runway is the most serious, while the 'dished' runway has the opposite effect. Undulating runways cause the most difficulties regarding compensating for Slope, as the variations in elevation can be numerous and also spread out. As the correcting data under discussion only covers two stages, averaging must be resorted to for each – i.e. the acceleration and deceleration elements of the runway must have their Slopes individually averaged. But at least the inaccuracies are isolated into two separate calculations and the total end value will be more accurate than that obtained by averaging the Slope for the whole runway, which is what happens if the Slope is calculated from the difference between the elevations of each threshold. Thus Fokker; in most other cases Slope is an *average* value and thus potentially inaccurate in many cases.

Wind Component
Finally, (e), or Wind Component. This is a *reported* value, and is thus

ADDITIONAL PERFORMANCE CONSIDERATIONS 105

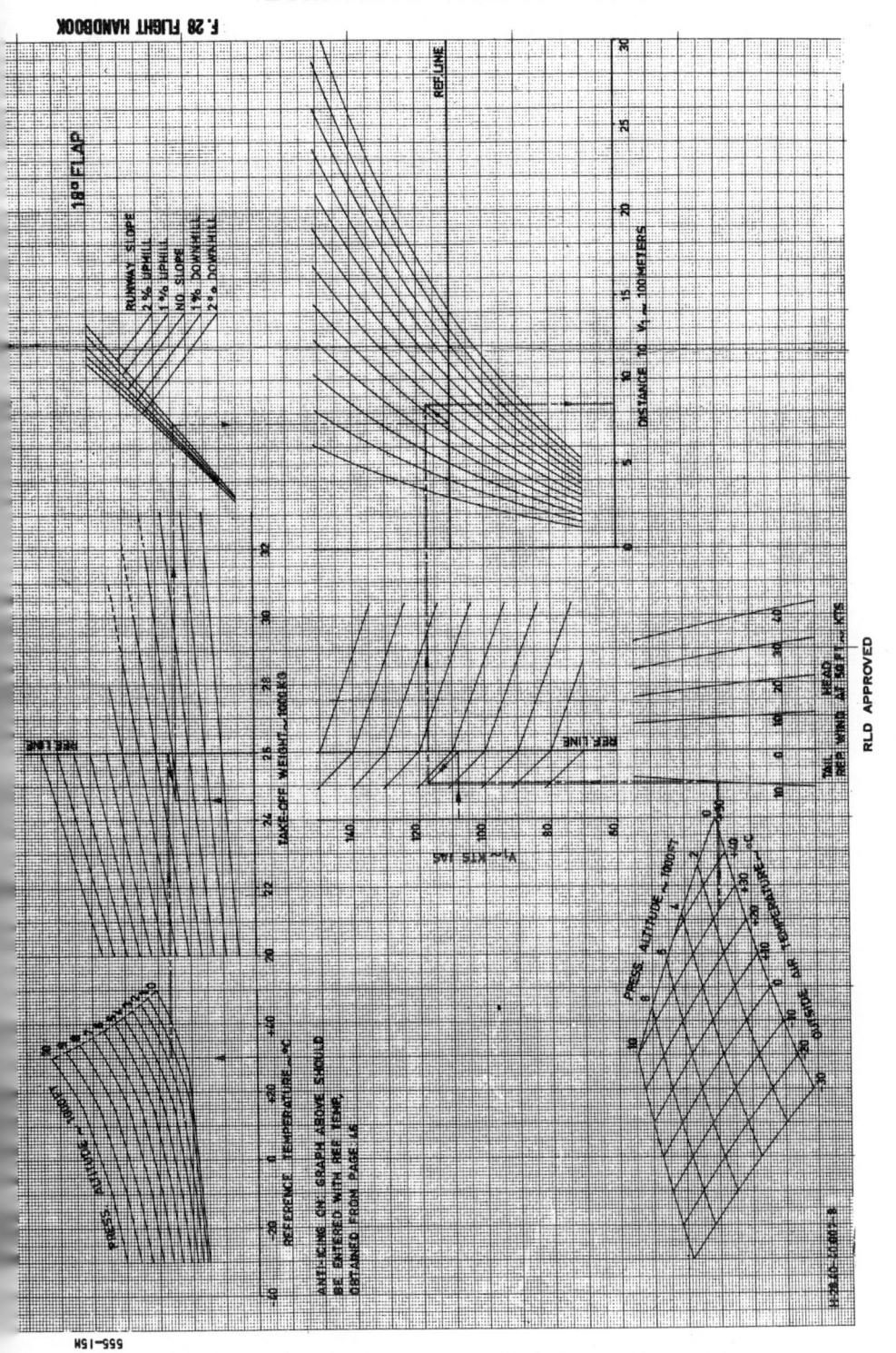

Fig. 8.1 A method of presenting distance required to reach V_1; the Fokker F28/4000

accurate at the time of reporting. In point of fact it is the Surface Wind Velocity that is reported; the flight crew convert this to a Wind Component relative to the runway. Unlike the case of Temperature, though, the Wind Component variable has room or potential for error. There is little that can be done to improve matters, though, as any errors will normally result from sudden changes in the Surface Wind Velocity. The point of measurement of the Surface Wind may not be strictly appropriate to the runway; on many airports the wind can vary at different points on the airport, due to geographical features, the effect of buildings, and so on. Wind is a very serious cause for concern in fact, due to a phenomenon known as Wind Shear. In a Horizontal Wind Shear the Surface Wind Speed and Direction, as reported, may suddenly and violently change to such a degree that even the 50%/150% factoring rule cannot contain the change. For example, a 20 kt Headwind Component can suddenly become a 70 kt Tailwind Component, without any warning either to those on the ground or the pilot. This Wind Shear can be a serious hazard, especially during the Landing, at the final stages. Imagine the effect on an aircraft approaching the flare when a 90 kt total Wind Component change through 180° is experienced. The ASI sensor, or probe, is detecting and presenting (in IAS, from EAS) a certain value in speed of the air mass relative to the aircraft. Suddenly this speed relationship is *reduced*, dramatically, by 90 kt. Let us assume that, in the final Landing Configuration the aircraft's Stalling Speed is 120 kt. The final approach speed will be 120 kt×1.3 ($1.3V_S$) = 156 kt. A 180° change in the air mass speed relative to the aircraft will result in this being reduced from 156 kt to 66 kt. (Due to inertia, the mass of the aircraft will be slow to accelerate so as to recover the relationship.) Unless this Wind Shear occurs at a high enough altitude on the approach to Landing the aircraft will stall, probably with catastrophic results. There have been many such accidents, in the main in the United States, and the FAA has undertaken very positive action to try and eliminate this problem. One method is to instal a number of Surface Wind sensors over the airport so that sudden approaching changes in the wind can be detected and reported to incoming aircraft in good time. Vertical Wind Shear which is at least as serious, is not directly connected with the runway Wind Component, and will therefore be left out of this matter so as to avoid misunderstandings. If conditions are favourable for producing Wind Shear it is some form of insurance, runway length permitting, to use as high an Approach speed as possible.

Takeoff Supplementary Instrumentation

Horizontal Wind Shear can be detected in the aircraft, if an accurate system that measures and displays Ground Speed (G/S) is available. At the time of writing no such system is known to be on the market, even though called for. Yet a system that can provide this facility, together with a facility for integrating speed and distance rolled has been built and flight tested, with satisfactory results. The designated authority in the United States for the investigation of aircraft accidents, the National Transportation Safety Board, NTSB, has also repeatedly called on the FAA to require the carriage of such a system, as the Appendices to this book will show. The system that was flight tested was, in fact, patented by the author of this book. Another system, having the same aim, but operating on a different basis, was also patented, in the United States by the sometime Chief of the Flight Standards Branch of the FAA. There is quite a story, and one worth recounting, attached to this matter.

As far as the author is concerned, the whole thing arose from a very simple beginning. This was the provision of Memory Indices – otherwise known as 'bugs', on the periphery of the Viscount aircraft's ASI. Their purpose was to mark the various significant speeds involved with the operation of this aircraft, and they were simply small plastic pointers that could be manually moved round the rim of the ASI. For our purposes, now under discussion, the significant positioning would be to mark V_1 and V_2. But, mused the author, would they not serve a far more valuable purpose if the V_1 'bug', at least, could provide an indication whether or not the Speed:Distance relationship was satisfactory. In fact, simply measure distance, and, if at V_1 or before, too much had been used the 'bug' glowed red, thus advising the pilot that the required performance level had not been met, and that the takeoff should be rejected. If, on the other hand, the distance consumed was equal to, or less than, that required, the 'bug' would glow green. A device was built, patented, and flight tested in the mid 1960s. Although the distance measuring capability was shown to be accurate – i.e. better than 1% error – there was a general resistance to its adoption, mainly on the grounds that the engineering problems were difficult, and that it was felt that it would cause too many unnecessarily aborted takeoffs. The NTSB/FAA activity in the United States had yet to come.

It became clear that, while the *principle* of the system described could not be disputed, the practice of its use was over-demanding and time-consuming. It was simple in construction, and in interpretation, but it relied on the availability and use of a Fokker-type Distance to V_1 chart in order to feed in the necessary distance. It also meant that there was no pre-warning of deterioration in the required performance level, although, at a further stage in the development process two pre-V_1 Speed:Distance 'bugs' were added, at fixed speed differences. But this failed to solve the cockpit workload problem, but in effect almost triplicated it. Figure 8.1 shows a typical Fokker Distance to V_1 chart; the layout shows how it is unsuited for use on the flight deck.

It was this sort of chart, though, together with the continuing development and miniaturisation of computers that pointed the way ahead for further development. Why not 'convert' the chart into a computer programme? On-board Flight Management Systems, FMS, based on small microprocessors, were coming into service, and it seemed logical to the author that either their capacity could be expanded so as to contain the takeoff performance of the aircraft type in which they were installed, or that a small, extra, computer dedicated to performance during takeoff and landing, could be provided that would interface with the FMS. Such a system was duly designed and patented by the author, who eventually succeeded in gaining financial support covering the building of a pre-prototype from a UK Government-constituted agency set up to finance British inventions. This was the National Research Development Corporation (NRDC), later to become the British Technology Group (BTG).

Then the problems started to begin. Naturally, before any airborne system may be put into commercial service in any civil aircraft, it must be approved by the appropriate certificating authority. This involves a suitable flight test programme; the funding provided did not run to the costs of such a programme. Neither could any Government agency agree to the provision of any flight test facility, even on a 'piggy-back' basis. The UK official airworthiness authority (initially the Air Registration Board, later to become part of the Civil Aviation Authority) showed polite interest, but little else. In fact, the view appeared to be that, while the ARB/CAA agreed with the principle, they thought that it could not be achieved. There were too many imponderables, such as described in (a) to (e) earlier in this chapter. Nevertheless, they gave their *qualified* encouragement.

The new system for Takeoff Monitoring was conceived shortly after a fatal takeoff accident in the United States in which an aircraft used grossly excessive distance to achieve V_1, without any engine malfunction. The crew had no means of knowing this and only rejected the takeoff when it became clear – all too late – that the aircraft was not going to become airborne before the end of the runway. (See Appendix (B).) The takeoff was aborted from a very high speed, above V_1, with substantial damage and many fatalities. The official US accident report recommended to the FAA that means should be developed so that flight crews should have a distance v speed relationship presented to them showing the progress of every takeoff. This was precisely what the author, and his colleagues, had set out to achieve.

Now comes an all too familiar story – at least, as regards the UK. With such a clear and categoric official recommendation to hand, the FAA was approached, as even then no support was forthcoming from UK sources, other than financial. The Takeoff Performance Indicating System, in conceptual form, was presented to the FAA, and that influential and respected body agreed without quibble to carry out a full in-flight evaluation of the system installed in a US Government Convair CV880M aircraft, without any charges. Convair were promptly contacted and willingly provided all the performance data for the aircraft needed to provide a computer programme. The system envisaged driving a 'bug' around the ASI dial by means of a servo motor, with a small computer controlling the 'bug's' position relative to the speed scale, by measuring distance. In other words, for the distance rolled the 'bug' was positioned continuously opposite the required speed. Distance rolled was measured by means of a small Doppler radar mounted in the wing-root of the aircraft. All that the pilot had to do was to key in the variables and then ensure that, up to V_1, the ASI pointer and the 'bug' remained aligned.

However, because of the various inaccuracies contained in the sub-paragraphs (a) to (e) earlier in this chapter (page 101), and also the slight variations of performance between different aircraft of the same type, a simple pointed 'bug' was too precise. If the ASI pointer lagged the 'bug' by even a knot or two a pilot could easily overreact, and unnecessarily abort the takeoff. So the 'bug' was replaced by a cursor, the leading edge being coloured green, followed by an amber 'caution' segment, and a red 'tail'. The cursor was proportioned so as to reflect an acceptable level of performance reduction *below* the level scheduled, so that takeoffs would be aborted only in those cases where the achieved level fell below the acceptable lower limit. The interpretation was simple, and came naturally; keep the ASI pointer in the green element and the takeoff was performing as scheduled. If it dropped into the amber sector it indicated that, up to the present, a *little* too much distance was being consumed for the IAS being achieved, but that there was nothing to worry about. Indeed, in many cases, restorative action could be taken. For example, if reduced thrust was being used this could be increased so as to try to bring the ASI pointer up to the green segment. But, if the pointer fell back far enough to lie within the red 'tail' the indication was clear – the acceleration to V_1 was seriously degraded, and unless the position could be restored rapidly *before* V_1 the takeoff should be abandoned (this was an advisory, and not a command, function). At the point when there was insufficient ASDA to abort the takeoff from the speed achieved (remembering, of course, that extra distance had been consumed in attaining the speed already), the performance cursor disappeared out of sight, thus advising the pilot that he had insufficient distance ahead in which to safely bring the aircraft to a halt. But, in the circumstances described, he had been given early, and continuous warning that he was using up excessive distance before reaching the V_1 point. (A photograph – Plate 8 – of the ASI display is provided that shows how the information was given.)

The results of the FAA evaluation, in which the author took part, showed that the system worked, and worked to a very high level of accuracy. In fact, the successful performance of the system was part of its shortfall; the FAA felt that there was further development potential and that this should be carried out before such a system could be made a mandatory requirement. Because of the availability of ground speed, as a by-function, coupled with the fact that the Doppler sensor could measure distance and ground speed when airborne from a height of some 3500 ft above ground level, the FAA felt

Plate 8 Takeoff Performance Monitor Prototype designed and tested by the US FAA with its designer (the author). (*Photograph courtesy of British Aerospace*)

that the device could be developed to detect the onset of horizontal wind shear, and also as a contribution to even more accurate automatic landings.

In spite of all this, an anti-performance monitoring movement built up, this consisting mainly of the commercial interests affected and not the pilots. In particular, certain aircraft manufacturers were sceptical, and airlines expected commercial benefits in exchange for the costs involved in fitting the system. The old bogey of such an instrument being likely to lead to a significantly increased number of aborted takeoffs once again reared its head, even though this was far from being the case. And once again the CAA joined in, echoing this last cry, and claiming that the variables that were accepted (i.e. (a) to (e)) could not be corrected out, so that the takeoff conditions could not accurately be inserted into the system prior to the takeoff. It is the author's opinion that this was not the case, and the CAA were given instances as to how the variables could be used as accurate data, instead of merely being a set of estimates, in the main. One example in which these arguments were disabused (with the exception of Temperature, which was measured accurately anyway, and Wind Component) was the case of All-up Weight. Weight and Balance Computers were on the market in the United States that measured the all-up weight and displayed this. There was no technical reason why the output from this computer could not be addressed to the Performance Computer, and thus the weight would no longer be an estimated value. The same went for airport altitude, and for Slope – all were disposed of as being arguments. But the CAA stuck to its viewpoint.

Fortunately, the FAA took a far more constructive attitude, and set up a widely based Committee to draw up a Specification for a Performance Monitoring system, covering mainly the takeoff and wind shear elements. This Committee submitted it's specification in late 1987 to the FAA, and at the time of writing the FAA is understood to be considering the matter constructively. But, to finalise this subject, the reader may be interested in a submission made to this Committee, prior to their finalising the Standard Specification. It may have even been guessed by now who was the originator of this submission. If this is so, and the guess was the CAA then it was 100% right. In fact, no other airworthiness authority appears to have made any submission. The CAA's case was the old, time-worn, doctrine. They submitted, in fact, that they supported the idea of takeoff performance monitoring but did not believe that this could be done. The old case of accounting for the variables was raised as being an insuperable obstacle. Why such a respected body should be so dogmatic is unknown. We can now only wait and see what moves the FAA will make. (The Committee has, in fact, issued a national Aerospace Standard for Takeoff Performance Monitoring Systems (TOPM) No. AS8044 dated August 1987.)

Irrespective of the outcome of the FAA's deliberations it remains the author's firm conviction that some form of takeoff performance monitoring must come soon. The principle cannot remain that the judging, and establishment, of such a critical and vital matter as the Decision Point can be left to an ASI reading alone. The clear evidence contained in the Appendices is justification alone for such 'radical' thinking, and the 'grey' areas described in (b) to (e) earlier in this chapter cannot be left as they are. At the very least they can be 'sharpened up'. It is certainly not the intention of the author to be a scaremonger in this connection, and it is accepted that the contingency of all of these variables being at the most adverse extent of their limits at the same time is pretty remote. But it *could* happen; a keener knowledge of the principles involved could help to reduce the likelihood.

Engine Instrument Indications

As will be seen in Appendix (C), crew liaison can be improved and thus help in the prevention of accidents. If something *appears* to be wrong then say so clearly and without ambiguity. Say *what* you think is wrong, urgently but calmly. If you find engine instrument readings that are not what you are accustomed to seeing, or expect to see, such as rpm or fuel flow for EPR appearing to be unusual, especially in marginal conditions, make up your mind and act quickly. *Stop and find out why.* It may be uncommercial, but so is a serious fatal accident. If your EPRs do not match up with your rpm then you have something wrong with the engine power output and you could well be close to disaster. Better to lose a few hundred pounds or dollars by abandoning the takeoff in good time than losing even one life. It may even be your own!

9: Small Airliners

No book on performance requirements is complete without some reference to the small airliners, or 'Feeder-liners', which are usually used to link small airports with the larger 'hubs', or to operate low density routes. Some scheduled routes for example, may be operated by aircraft with as few as eight passenger seats, with a frequency that is dictated by traffic demand. Such aircraft are still subject to performance requirements, but these are much simpler than those for the larger transport-category airliner.

It is felt that some reference should be made to certain requirements that cover the performance of 'small' airliners. That is to say, Public Transport aircraft having a Maximum All-up Weight not exceeding 5700 kg. There are, as yet, no Joint Airworthiness Requirements (JARs) published to cover this category of aircraft. There are, therefore, only FARs, (FAR 23) and BCARs to consider, and these are not dissimilar. FAR 135 is of some interest, though, in that it permits a low speed overrun of the runway in the event of an aborted takeoff. Apart from this concession, in United States regulation, no acceleration-stop data is scheduled in either FARs or BCARs and therefore V_1 does not appear. The takeoff is regulated by the Takeoff Run (TOR) and the Takeoff Distance (TOD), associated with a Takeoff Safety Speed. WAT is also applicable.

In this chapter we will deal with the UK requirements only, and to be more specific, those contained in the Air Navigation (General) Regulations as amended, of 1981, and also BCARs Section K. Certain non-performance requirements arise in the UK Air Navigation Order that perhaps should be mentioned, in that eventually they affect one performance aspect. The reference is contained in ANO Article 18, and concerns the number of pilots that must be carried. This Article is a bit woolly, and concerns itself with such things as the type and number of engines – e.g. piston, turbo-prop, or jet – whether or not the aircraft is pressurised, and whether or not an autopilot is fitted. Basically, for this category of aircraft – e.g. a Twin Otter – the ANO Art. 18 (3)(b)(iii) specifies that, as from January 1, 1990, at least two pilots shall be carried (if more than nine passengers are to be carried). At present, i.e. at the time of writing, such aircraft require only one pilot to be carried. The two pilot requirement is specified to cover those circumstances where compliance with Instrument Flight Rules (IFR) is required. This, of course, clearly means 100% of commercial operations, as it is not really practicable to base an operation on permanent Visual Flight Rules.

Net Flight Path – Second Segment
There has been, for a long time, a restriction on one Performance aspect that would appear to be linked to this new legislation, and this is to be found in the Net Flight Path requirements. To be specific, this concerns the Second Segment, with all-engines operating. (The Net Flight Path requirements will be gone into in more detail later in this chapter.) But, in the context of the matter now under discussion, the current BCARs Section K require that the all-engines operating Second Segment must have a lower altitude limit at the reported Cloud Ceiling, while the upper limit is either 1500 ft *or* the Maximum Takeoff Power time limit. Power failure *must* be assumed to occur at the Cloud Ceiling, and this is due to the inadvisability of there being merely one pilot to cope with an asymmetric power situation alone, and also have to fly an accurate flight path for terrain clearance reasons. Once again, no commercial operation can be predicated on the pious hope that there will not be a Cloud Ceiling below 1500 ft, and therefore any such operation must be based on IFR conditions throughout the Net Flight Path.

Now to Performance requirements, and these will be taken in logical order. First, WAT. At the altitude of the takeoff surface, at V_2, all engines operating, undercarriage up where applicable, flaps at takeoff setting, and power at Maximum Takeoff, the Gross gradient of climb must be not less than 5%, or the rate of climb not less than 400 fpm. The Second Segment assumes that the undercarriage is fully retracted (if applicable), and that the flaps are fully retracted at 200 ft altitude; power is Maximum Takeoff. The Gross Performance is based on a climb at V_2; Net performance is the Gross Performance diminished by 2% for the all-engines case, and 0.8% for an engine out, with the remainder at Maximum Takeoff Power.

Where the stalling speed of an aircraft in the *Landing* configuration exceeds 60 kt (V_{S_0}) the Gross gradient of climb may not be less than zero, with the speed at V_2, Flaps at Takeoff setting, undercarriage up (if applicable), the Critical engine inoperative and the remainder at Maximum Takeoff Power. (K2-4. (2.5) refers.)

The Takeoff ground roll and runway requirements do not make any provision for a Decision Point and Speed (V_1). Instead, the Takeoff Distance Required (TODA) is the gross distance multiplied by 1.25 from the start of the takeoff to a Screen height of 50 ft. (As against a 30 ft Screen for Transport Category aircraft.) The Takeoff Run Required (TORA) is the gross distance from the start of the takeoff to the point at which V_2 is reached, with the aircraft on or near the ground, multiplied by 1.15. Two techniques may be scheduled, these being for a 'Normal' takeoff and a Short field takeoff. In the first case the aircraft is accelerated on or near the ground until, in the event of an engine failure, directional control will be such that the resulting 'swing' at V_{EF} will not exceed 30 ft. Speed V_2 (Takeoff Safety Speed) must be attained by the 50 ft Screen Height point. In the Short Field case the aircraft is accelerated on or near the ground until V_{MCA} is achieved, with V_2 being achieved within 10 seconds of V_{LOF}. In the event of V_{EF} occurring at speeds below V_2 it must be possible to land ahead. BCARs Section K2-3, 4, and 7 refer.

It will be seen, therefore, that there is some form of contingency built in to the scheduled performance for takeoff. The control requirements, and the ability to re-land ahead, apply to both takeoff techniques, and are defined in BCARs Section K2-7.3.3 and 3.4. What is *not* defined, though, is the distance available that is required to re-land ahead, if this becomes necessary.

The Net Flight Path is scheduled from the 50 ft Screen Height up to at least 1500 ft. The takeoff is assumed to be that applicable to normal techniques, but a 'Short Field' technique may be scheduled if appropriate. The data thus scheduled must be for all-engines operating, and may also be scheduled so as to cover the one engine out case if required. (K2-3) (4.1) refers.)

The Net Flight Path, with all-engines operating, is the Gross Flight Path, diminished by a climb gradient of 2.0%, or its equivalent in any Acceleration segment (4.2 (a)). The Net Flight Path for the engine out case is the Gross Flight Path, diminished by a climb gradient of 0.8% or its equivalent in any Acceleration segment. The conditions for establishing Gross performance are as follows:

For Normal takeoff techniques the Gross performance is determined from the 50 ft Screen up to a height of at least 200 ft, at which the Flaps are retracted to the en route setting – i.e. fully retracted. (The 'en route setting' is merely official jargon for 'fully retracted' – unless there is some strange aircraft around that flies en route with some flap out. If so, one wonders why the wing planform was not designed so as to reflect this configuration.) During this element the speed must be V_2, and undercarriage retraction selected at a height of 50 ft.

From the flap retraction height, up to a height of 1500 ft, the aircraft is climbed at a speed V_2, with the flaps at 'the appropriate setting'.

For the Short field takeoff technique the Net Flight Path starts at the 50 ft Screen Height, with speed V_2 being attained as described in the Takeoff paragraph above, and using the procedure described. Where applicable, undercarriage retraction is selected at V_2. Flap retraction may not be initiated below a height of 200 ft, and the climb to 1500 ft is made at the speed V_2.

The power setting for both techniques is Maximum Takeoff power, up to the time limit for such power, and then Maximum Continuous Power (MCP).

Note
The all-engines operating climb out performance may not be extended above the Cloud Ceiling (Cloud Base). Once this height is reached, one engine *must* be *assumed* to fail and the pre-takeoff Net Flight Path calculation must be based on this assumption. Normally one engine inoperative conditions are assumed, as mentioned earlier, from a height of 200 ft above the runway, when flap retraction also takes place. (K2-3. (4.2.1) refers.)

BCARs Section K do not specify a Net Flight Path profile by the number of segments required. However, Sub-section K7-5 Appendix 4 provides details of up to four elements, or Segments; some Flight Manuals may show data for five segments, including a horizontal Acceleration Segment at a height of 400 ft. All Net Flight Path segments assume that the flight is taking place in IFR. The Segments defined in BCARs K7-5 Appendix 4 are as follows:

First Segment. This segment extends from the end of the TODR up to a height of 200 ft, at which height the undercarriage is assumed to have been retracted (unless this is fixed, such as is the case with the Twin Otter, Trislander, etc.), and the speed attained is the Takeoff Safety Speed for flap retraction, upon which the flaps are retracted. All-engines are operating.

Second Segment. This segment extends from the end of the First segment up to a height of *either* 1500 ft with all-engines operating or the height at which V_{EF} has been assumed.

Third segment. This segment extends from the assumed power failure point and ends at a height of 1500 ft or the Maximum Takeoff Power Limit point (usually 5 minutes after brake-release), whichever comes first. (One engine inoperative.)

Fourth segment. This segment is for the 'slow-climber'. It starts at the

5 minute power limit point for Maximum Takeoff Power, *where this occurs before a height of 1500 ft can be attained,* and ends at 1500 ft. One engine is assumed to be inoperative throughout this segment.

The 'Five Minute Point' is the point on the Net Flight Path, 5 minutes from brake-release, and with an engine failure assumed to have taken place at the prevailing cloud base. Or, in practical terms, 200 ft. Once a height of 1500 ft has been attained the en route conditions apply.

At a height of 1500 ft the en route requirements are scheduled. Firstly, the required speed is defined; this may not be less than the speed that is appropriate to the 1500 ft height, with one engine inoperative, as scheduled for the Net Flight Path. The effect of Weight at the time – i.e. instantaneous weight – may be allowed for alone, and no credit may be taken for pressure or temperature changes. The all-engines operating ceiling must be established from the all-engines operating data. This ceiling is the altitude at which the *pressure* rate of climb falls to 150 ft/minute minimum. The one engine out data for the en route case is Net, and is the gross gradient of climb available diminished by 1%.

The Drift-down to Stabilising Altitude is determined from the one engine out Net data scheduled in the same way as described for larger aircraft in Chapter 6. The en route requirements are defined in BCARs K2-4 (3).

Baulked Landing Requirements
The Baulked Landing requirements, following a descent from cruising altitude, call for a gross gradient of climb of not less than 3.2%, with the engines (all-engines operating) at a power that is attainable from the initiation of the Baulked Landing with engines at flight idle, after 5 seconds maximum time lag. The Flaps can be either in the Landing setting or that setting at which they could assume 5 seconds after the initiation of the procedure (this allows for the Baulked Landing being initiated at a height sufficient to at least partially retract the flaps). The Speed must not be less than $1.2V_{S_0}$ nor greater than $1.3V_{S_0}$. The undercarriage is assumed to be extended. Section K2-4. (2.6) refers.

Landing Distance Requirements
The Landing Distance requirement is specified, like the takeoff, for both normal and short field procedures. The all-engines operating required Landing Distance is the Measured Landing Distance for all-engines operating, multiplied by 1.43. A conventional Approach to

the 50 ft height point is assumed, with a gradient of descent not exceeding 5% (3° Glide Path). (The Landing Distance is measured from the 50 ft Screen (height) point and then multiplied by 1.43.) Either the all-engines, or the one engine inoperative distance may be scheduled, and the aircraft configuration must be that appropriate to the number of engines operating. All available means of retardation may be used. For short landing techniques it is required that, should an engine fail during the Approach it must be possible to continue the Approach and land safely. Screen heights of less than 50 ft may be scheduled for this technique. For the one engine out landing case, only the normal technique is permitted. In this instance the Measured Landing Distance is multiplied by 1.2 to give the Landing Distance Required. Normally all Flight Manuals will contain this factoring upwards and will state this. Section K2-5 (3) and (4) refer.

Appendix A
Worked Example in Outline
(BAe 146–100)

The method of calculating the Maximum permissible Takeoff Weight is outlined below, by stages, and is shown schematically by means of the accompanying flow chart (Fig. A.1).

Stages
1. Assemble all known, or anticipated data, into two groups:
   (a) Airport Altitude, Temperature (°C), Wind Component, and proposed Flap setting and
   (b) TODA (m), ASDA, TORA, and Slope (%).

2. From group (a) obtain the WAT limited weight. This may be due to either the available climb gradient in the First and Second Segments alone, or it may also include an additional limit (Tyre Speed) as a result of using low pressure 160 mph tyres, due to runway bearing strength considerations. If the standard 190 mph tyres are fitted then the WAT limited weight is only a function of altitude and temperature. Make a note of the weight resulting from WAT.

3. Using TODA and ASDA find the resulting 'D' value, and $V_1:V_R$ ratio (see Fig. 3.2). Using TORA and ASDA repeat this process, using the appropriate Flight Manual chart (not reproduced).

   Using TORA and TODA find the 'D' value for the all-engines operating case ($V_1:V_R$ is not involved).

   Take the lowest 'D' value, and associated $V_1:V_R$ and note this. If this 'D' value is the all-engines case then use the $V_1:V_R$ associated with the next lowest 'D' – i.e. TODA/ASDA or TORA/ASDA. Using the limiting 'D' value establish the runway limited TOW and note. (See Fig. 3.3.)

4. Check for any Brake Energy limit that may affect the value of $V_1:V_R$ noted. If not limiting then the *lowest* weight recorded for stage 2 or stage 3 is the RTOW for carrying forward. If Brake Energy *does* limit, then the optimum weight for V_{MBE} and $V_1:V_R$ must be calculated. To do this draw a vertical scale for the ratio on a sheet of graph paper against a horizontal scale for weight. Plot the limiting weight brought forward from stages 2 and 3 against $V_1:V_R$. Now reduce the ASDA available quite arbitrarily by some amount

Fig. A.1 Takeoff calculation flow chart

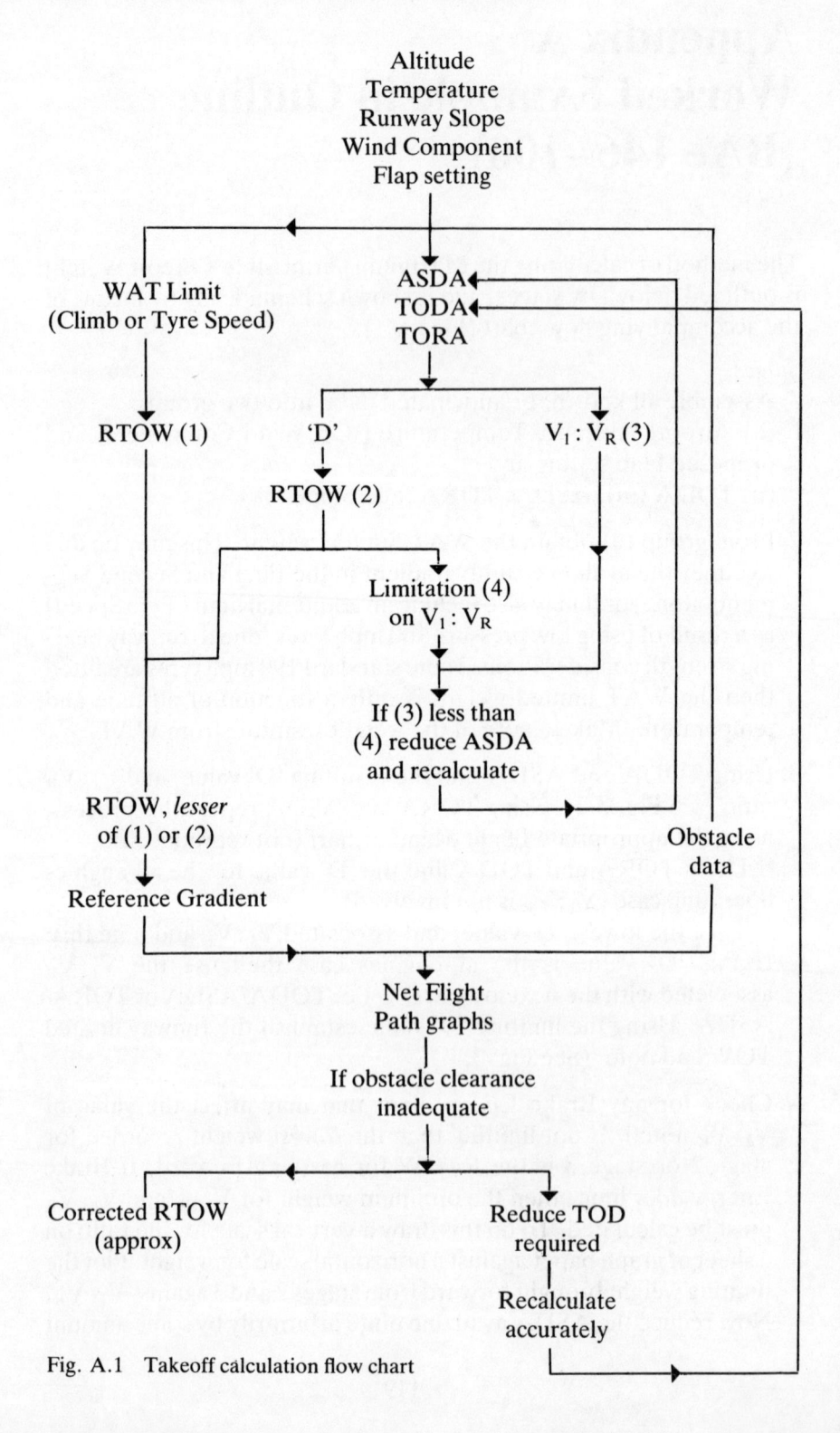

– say 200 m – 3 or 4 times, and plot the resulting weight reductions (having recalculated these) against $V_1:V_R$ (also recalculated). Plot this line on the graph grid. Note how weight *reduces* with ASDA reduction.

Now, reading from the Flight Manual $V_1:V_R$ limit chart, and using the weights just found, with their $V_1:V_R$ ratios, plot a second line. Note how the $V_1:V_R$ value for V_{MBE} *rises* with decreased weight.

Where the two lines just plotted intersect, is the weight as limited by Brake Energy limits together with its associated $V_1:V_R$. Note these values.

5 The Maximum permissible weight is now the *lowest* of WAT, Tyre speed, or Brake Energy limited weights found in stages 2, 3, and 4. Carry this weight, and ratio, forward

6 Next check for obstacle clearance (assuming that obstacles are present) using the Flight Manual Flight Path graphs and the RTOW found above. Initially find the Reference Gradient and check this against any known obstacles relative to the beginning of the Takeoff Flight Path. If found to be limiting, reduce the TODA and find a new weight and $V_1:V_R$ until the required obstacle clearance is achieved.

7 Now recalculate, using this final weight, and obtain the appropriate $V_1:V_R$ value. From this, and for the RTOW thus calculated, find the values V_1, V_R, and V_2 from the Flight Manual chart portraying these values. (See Fig. 3.4.)

The process described is normally somewhat simpler as the majority of runways are rarely affected by Flight Path considerations. Normally TODA/ASDA will control the RTOW although TORA and the all-engines TODA may come into the picture. At high altitudes and temperatures WAT may override. In the case of the BAe 146–100 normally 190 mph tyres are fitted and these do not produce any Tyre Speed limit. If the value of $V_1:V_R$ due to V_{MBE} limit is *greater* than that found from the 'D' charts then the latter value applies, as there is no $V_1:V_R$ nor Brake Energy limit.

Regrettably it is not possible, due to editorial and production reasons, to reproduce all the Flight Manual charts necessary to illustrate this example.

Appendix B
Accident to DC-8-63 at Anchorage, 1970

This is an analysis of an accident report by the United States National Transportation Safety Board (NTSB) into a DC-8-63F (N4409C) accident at Anchorage, Alaska, on November 27, 1970. (The NTSB is the competent investigating authority for aviation accidents in the United States.) This accident is closely performance-related, and no engine failure was involved. It concerns an attempted takeoff in conditions of freezing drizzle, prior to which the aircraft had been competently de-iced. The *estimated* weight for the takeoff was 349 012 lb (158 311 kg), and the maximum permissible takeoff weight was structurally limited to 350 000 lb (158 759 kg). So the aircraft was below its Maximum TOW, and there were no WAT or runway limitations; the aircraft was in a fit condition for takeoff. The significant takeoff speeds were: V_1–138 kt, V_R–153 kt, and V_2–163 kt. (All speeds IAS.)

From the captain's account the initial acceleration, up to some 130 kt or so, appeared to be normal and there was no discernible trend towards reduction in acceleration. After 130 kt, though, the acceleration appeared to 'flatten out'. V_1 was attained, and the decayed acceleration previously noticed disappeared; the aircraft continued its acceleration to 145 kt. At around this speed the acceleration dropped off again, but there appeared to be plenty of runway available ahead.

V_R was reached and the aircraft was rotated at a point *estimated* to be some 1500 to 1800 ft from the end of the runway. *After passing the runway end some roughness was noticed,* and the tail appeared to be dragging. The captain then decided to abort the takeoff from above V_R, and beyond the runway limits, having deemed this to be the safest course of action. It is of interest to note that the first officer thought that it took longer than normal to reach V_1 but because of the amount of runway ahead, was not unduly worried. He testified that he had checked the engine instruments several times up to V_1 and that all were reading normally. Although noting a reduction in acceleration after V_1 the first officer remained unperturbed, as he still thought that there was enough runway ahead to accelerate to V_R and to takeoff.

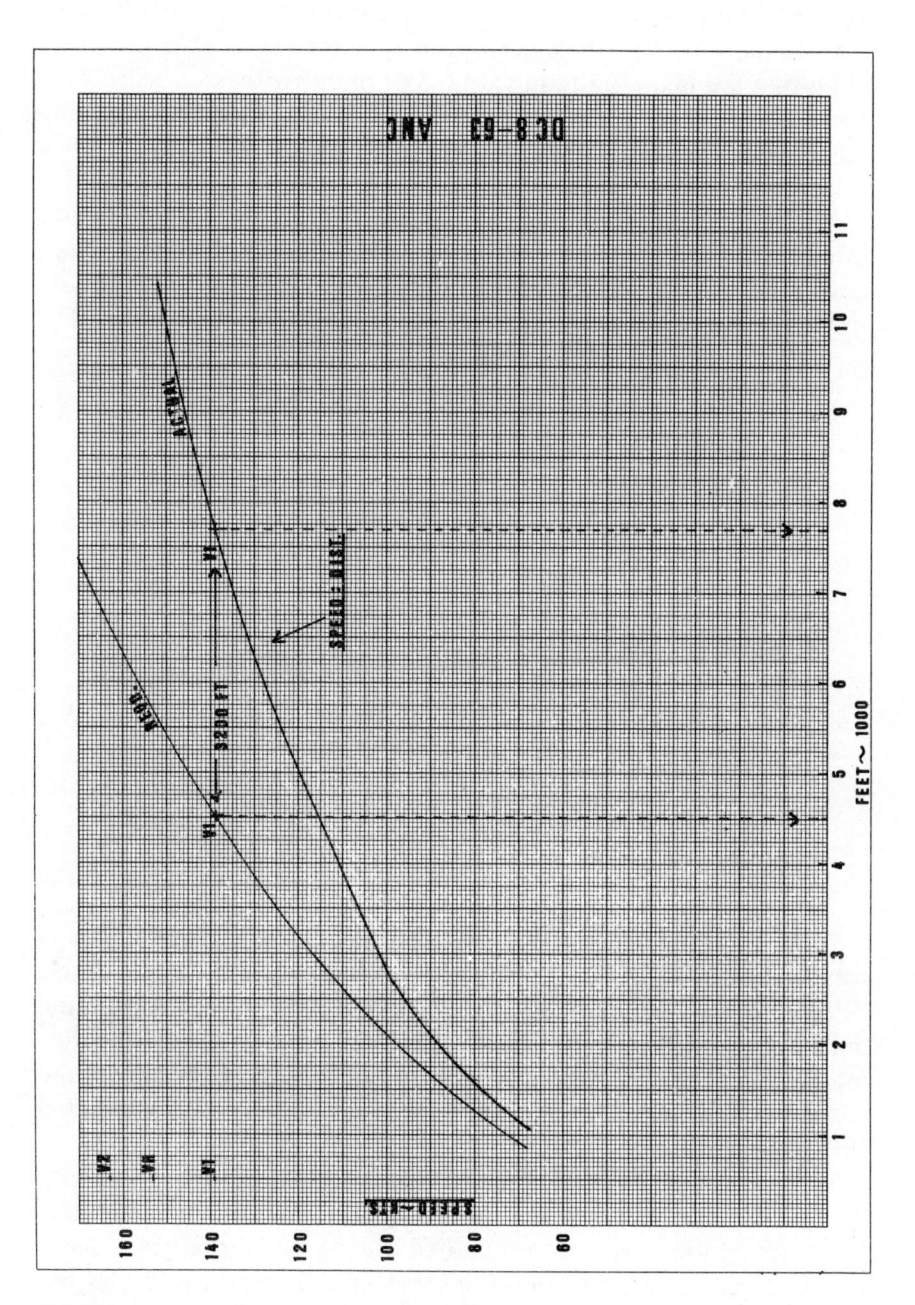

Fig. B.1 A fatal accident, where the acceleration achieved was drastically below that required

124   HANDBOOK OF AIRCRAFT PERFORMANCE

Even at V_R itself he still thought that there was enough runway available. He, too, noted roughness after rolling off the end of the runway. (To the author, at least, this does not appear to be at all surprising!)

During the takeoff attempt a number of eye witnesses heard what they thought were tyres bursting. Two US Air Force (USAF) pilot passengers also heard what they thought were tyres bursting, during the ground roll.

The Flight Data Recorder (FDR) showed that the maximum IAS attained was 152 kt and that this was reached in approximately 72 seconds after the start of the takeoff. After this a rapid deceleration set in. A number of Speed v Time readings were available from the FDR tape. These may be tabulated thus:

IAS – kt	Time from Start – seconds
80	25
100	35
120	45
139 (V_1)*	59
152	72

*An earlier figure quoted in the text of the Report gives V_1 as being 138 kt.
It is not felt that one knot here would account for anything significant.

In the resulting overrun at such a high speed the aircraft was almost totally destroyed by fire, with the exception of part of the wings. Forty-seven people died, out of 229 on board. There was substantial and conclusive evidence to support the reports of tyres bursting during the roll down the runway; pieces of tyre were scattered down the runway for a distance of 5000 to 6000 ft. There were also associated skid marks.

We now turn to the Performance aspects, and these are very significant. After the accident the takeoff was re-enacted by computer, using actual measured data obtained during the aircraft type flight test programme, and the conditions that actually prevailed during the attempted takeoff – i.e. Weight, Flap setting, Slope, *Barometric* pressure, Wind velocity, Temperature, and EPR.

The following Table shows the Performance level that *should* have been attained.

APPENDIX B   125

The conditions were:
Weight 349 012 lb
Flaps 23°
Slope −0.28%
Barometric Pressure 29.97 in Hg W/V 060/6 kt
Temperature 24°F
EPR 1.86

Speed – kt IAS	Time – seconds	Distance – feet
V_1 – 139	39.2	4500
V_R – 153.3	44.5	5700
V_{LO} – 163	48.0	6600

and

Distance – feet	Time – seconds	Speed – kt IAS
1000	18.0	72.4
2000	25.7	98.3
3000	31.7	117.2
4000	36.9	132.4
5000	41.5	145.5
6000	45.6	156.8
7000	49.5	167.3

Now, the accident's *achieved* performance, from the FDR:

Distance – feet	Time – seconds	Speed – kt IAS
1250	22.0	72.4
2650	33.0	98.3
4700	45.0	117.2
6600	55.0	132.4
7700	60.0	139.0 (V_1)
8800	65.0	145.4

126 HANDBOOK OF AIRCRAFT PERFORMANCE

Comparing the computed – i.e. expected – distance:time:speed values against the achieved figures we find the following results:

Required Distance – feet	Achieved Distance – feet	Required Time – seconds	Achieved Time – seconds
1000	1250	18	22
2000	2650	25.7	33
3000	4700	31.7	45
4000	6600	36.9	55
4500 (V_1 point)	7700	39.2	60
5000	8800	41.5	65
5584	10 400	44.0	72
5700	–	44.5	–

In the cold light of historic and measured analysis it is startlingly clear that there was a shortfall in performance that may be referred to as being horrific. In fact, for the last achieved, *and recorded*, distance:time:speed relationship *nearly twice the required distance* had been consumed. The aircraft had rolled 10 400 ft when it should have only used 5584 ft. At the V_1 *point* the required distance was 4500 ft; 7700 ft were, in fact, used, this being no less than 3200 ft too much. At 98.3 kt it had consumed some 32.5% excess runway already, and had taken 28.6% longer than required in terms of time. Figure B1 shows the required v achieved speed:distance relationship graphically.

During the ground roll the crew noticed nothing *seriously* amiss until the last few seconds, when the end of the runway came up. Then, and only then, did it become clear that the acceleration had become drastically degraded, and the only discernible symptom of trouble – i.e. rough-rolling – became apparent. But how *could* the crew have been aware that something was amiss – they had reached the sacrosanct V_1 IAS value without engine failure, after all. There were no engine instrumentation anomalies at all, other than that the N_2 (Compressor rpm), Fuel flow, and EGT (Exhaust Gas Temperature) indicators for No 1 engine were reading incorrectly due to a defect in that engine's EPR system. This defect was known beforehand, and it was, apparently, an allowable deficiency. The required takeoff power for No 1 engine was set by aligning the instruments referred to above, manually by throttle, to correspond with the readings for the other three engines, as was permissible.

In the investigation's report the crew were totally exonerated from any blame. The most likely cause of the accident was that (a) the aircraft's brake system had malfunctioned, *or* the Parking Brake had inadvertently been applied, as a result of which *all* main wheels had locked when lining-up for takeoff (but no evidence was found to support the Parking Brake possibility). (b) This was in association with an ice covered runway. The aircraft most probably *slid*, as opposed to rolled, the whole length of the runway, with all mainwheel tyres progressively bursting during the run – if that is the right word for it. The resulting frictional Drag not surprisingly caused an excessive reduction in the acceleration level. But this was a night takeoff, and the crew had no means whatsoever of knowing about this reduced acceleration level, nothing in the way of performance monitoring being available to them. Although not mentioned in the report, one wonders if, had this been a daylight takeoff, the poor acceleration might have become more obvious?

On March 29, 1972 the NTSB Report was issued, and amongst its recommendations was that the FAA should 'Determine and implement takeoff procedures that will provide the flight crew with time or distance reference to appraise the aircraft's acceleration to the V_1 speed.'

So, here we have clear evidence that the V_1 concept was lacking and that only in the case of engine failure *recognition* in good time was it valid. How could it be of *any* relevance in the case of a takeoff in which all engines were operating at the required EPR? An engine failure can be detected without too much trouble. But, at that time, performance degradation due to other causes could not. Incidentally, no explanation could be found for the fact that the brakes had, it appeared, locked on. They were operating normally during the taxi-out. But it seemed to be certain that locked on they were, for all the main wheel rims were worn down to flat surfaces.

NTSB Report No. AAR-72-12 refers.

Appendix C
Accident to B737 at Washington DC, 1982

This analysis is based on an accident report by the United States NTSB, following on an investigation into a fatal accident by a Boeing 737-222 (N62AF) in Washington DC on January 13, 1982. The Report was published on August 10, 1982. It concerns a takeoff from Washington National Airport in extremely adverse conditions, although these were not stringent enough to prevent operations. A feature common to the conditions that existed in the case described in Appendix (B) was icing; in the accident analysed in Appendix (B) the precipitation was freezing rain, while in the case now under review it was snow. Nevertheless, like the earlier accident, it should have been avoidable, and likewise no engine failure occurred. It again highlights the deficiencies inherent in the V_1 concept – indeed, it may be said that the apparent sanctity of this principle was substantially a contributory factor towards the circumstances that caused the accident. The attainment of V_1, with no engine failure, led the Captain to believe that all was well. In fact, everything was very far from being well, as was shown by a very thorough and detailed analysis of the Cockpit Voice Recorder, (CVR) and the FDR tapes.

The accident was unusual in that the aircraft became airborne but then rapidly assumed a nose-high attitude and developed a noticeable rate of sink, rather than climb. The aircraft had, by then, left the airport boundary and was, in fact, over the River Potomac which borders the airport. In just over a minute from Brake release the aircraft struck a busy road bridge crossing the river. 78 people were killed – 74 from the aircraft and four in cars on the bridge.

The conditions that were calculated pre-takeoff were: *Estimated* Takeoff Weight, 102 300 lb, within the Maximum Structural Weight of 109 000 lb – i.e. the RTOW was, *by estimate,* because of the approved practice of the use of Standard weights, some 6700 lb below the Maximum permitted takeoff weight. V_1 was 137 kt, V_R was 139 kt, and V_2 was 144 kt. The two knots difference between V_1 and V_R would indicate a very high $V_1:V_R$ ratio, and this would seem to show that the runway was not limiting. All speeds quoted are IAS; the aircraft was in all respects fully serviceable and fit for takeoff.

The weather conditions were bad, but not prohibitive. About three minutes before the crash the following *reported* values were recorded: Cloud Ceiling (CC): 200 ft, sky obscured. Visibility: ½ mile. Weather: Moderate snow. Temperature: 24° F. Wind velocity (W/V): 010°/11 kt. Altimeter: 29.94 in. Hg. Runway Visual Range (RVR): 2800 ft to 3500 ft.

About 13 minutes later the reported values were: CC 200 ft, sky obscured. Visibility: 3/8 mile. Weather: Moderate snow. Temperature: 24°F. W/V: 020°/13. Altimeter: 29:91 in. Hg. RVR: 2000 ft to 3500 ft.

The aircraft had been de-iced overall some 50 minutes before Brake Release, and no further decontamination action took place, even though snow was noted on the aircraft's structure. Pushback from the Terminal took place some 36 minutes before Brake Release time. As it was snowing throughout this period there would certainly have been further accretion.

From the CVR recording it was noted that, just over 20 minutes before Brake Release time, the flight crew were discussing the advisability of further de-icing. The first officer commented that some time had elapsed since they were last de-iced. The captain then said he had a 'little' snow on his wing – i.e. the wing on his side of the aircraft – to which the first officer replied that he had about ¼ inch on his side. After Brake Release the first officer commented on certain discrepancies, but *failed to specify what these were*. It seems clear, now, that certain engine instrument readings were disturbing him. The captain, however, was then concentrating on his ASI readings and brushed aside his first officer's concern, on the grounds that he (the captain) was noting satisfactory *speed* readings. Note the utter faith in indicated *speed* readings. Some two seconds after V_2 the CVR recorded the sound of the Stick-shaker (Stall warning device) operating. From this it may be assumed that, although the aircraft was some 20% above its scheduled stalling speed – (V_2 minimum = $1.2V_S$) – the aircraft was, in fact, very close to the stall. Remember the noticeable nose-high pitch attitude mentioned earlier?

It should be noted that, owing to the deaths of the flight crew in this accident, no evidence from them was available. However, the CVR tape provided a source of evidence that was very valuable indeed. Now take careful note – what *was* missing, though, was identification of what was causing the first officer concern. Had he spoken out firmly and clearly, identifying the apparent problem, he and 77 other people might still be alive.

A significant piece of information was provided by the FDR tape. After liftoff the climb IAS reduced slightly, from 147 kt to 144 kt – V_2, in fact. But, within seconds the IAS had decayed rapidly, from 144 kt to 130 kt. Or, in other words, from V_2 to seven knots *below* V_1. And bear in mind that there had been no engine failure.

It will now be apposite to list the engine instrumentation, which was mounted logically in the centre panel. These instruments were mounted in two vertical rows, there being one row per engine. Starting from the top each row consisted of:

(a) N_1 rpm indicator (Low pressure compressor speed)
(b) EPR indicator (Engine Pressure Ratio, being the Exit:Inlet pressure. EPR is the primary engine power indication)
(c) EGT indicator (Exhaust Gas Temperature)
(d) N_2 rpm indicator (High pressure compressor speed)
(e) Fuel flow indicator (Fuel consumption rate lb/hour)

The importance of these instrument readings will become apparent as the analysis proceeds.

Ingenious testing was carried out by the NTSB, both by laboratory simulation and also by means of tests with a similar Type and Variant of the 737, in conjunction with the aircraft manufacturer, – Boeing. The first piece of ingenuity was the discovery that the CVR could pick up the sound frequency of the engines, and the NTSB had already developed, after considerable research, a formula for measuring N_1 rpm by conversion from the audio frequency as recorded by the CVR. This testing provided the important clue that the engine rpm at N_1 were not what they should have been.

More tests carried out in conjunction with Boeing shed further light on the mystery – again with great ingenuity. The required EPR for the accident takeoff conditions was 2.04. The inlet Pt_2 probe of one engine was deliberately blocked for the tests and that engine throttle was then set so as to give an EPR reading of 2.04. The N_1, N_2, EGT, and Flow readings were then noted. The other engine – i.e., the one with the unblocked probe – was then adjusted by throttle to give engine instrument readings to match those for the probe-blocked engine. With matching engine instrumentation, except for EPR, the evidence emerged clearly – with identical N_1 and N_2, EGT, and Flow readings for both engines the EPR for the unblocked-probe engine read only 1.70. The throttle was then adjusted so as to bring the EPR up to 2.04, to match the other engine, and the instrument readings were then noted. The angular differences between the pointers for each pair of instruments were noted, and revealing. These angular differences were as follows: N_1: 30°. EGT: 20°. N_2: 15°. and Flow: 42°. Were these angular discrepancies the thing that concerned the first officer so much? It should be borne in mind that, in the case of the crashed aircraft, both rows of instruments would have been giving similar readings – always assuming that *both* Pt$_2$ probes were blocked. If this was the case then the only suspicious indications would have been that all the pointers were not where they should have been, and were actually reading low by the amounts of the angular differences noted above. Was the first officer sensing, in fact, that the pointers were not where he expected them to be normally?

Let us list the *readings* for the engines in actual terms:

	Pt$_2$ blocked Actual EPR: 1.70	Pt$_2$ unblocked Actual EPR: 2.04
N$_1$	79%*	91%
EPR	2.04	2.04
EGT	387°*	455°
N$_2$	85%	90%
Flow	5550 lb/hr*	8100 lb/hr

*These indications were very substantially below those to be expected.

Further tests showed that the Thrust per engine at 1.70 EPR was about 10 750 lb, against the expected value of 14 500 lb. A substantial shortfall in any terms.

The engine Pt$_2$ probe is mounted in the eye of the engine nose fairing, while that for Pt$_7$ is mounted aft of the turbine section. The Pt$_2$ probe was already known to be prone to icing (for the aircraft type), but application of engine de-icing would also de-ice this probe. But, from the CVR tape reading it was believed that the engine de-icing was *not* selected On. This in falling snow and an OAT of 24°(F)! With the Pt$_2$ sensor blocked, the EPR instrumentation then 'read' the pressure inside the fairing – a lower value than outside, but enough to give a plausible EPR reading. (For example, if the nose sensor were to be *totally* inoperative then, in theory anyway, the Pt$_7$ sensor would have no source of comparison.) To have a ratio two values are necessary and both must be accurate. In the case under discussion there was enough of a reading to permit power to be produced that 'claimed' to be 2.04 EPR but which was, in fact, only 1.70 EPR, due to the comparison being effected against an inaccurate value.

Further tests established that the B737 variant in question, under the various conditions that applied at the time of the accident, should have reached V$_{LOF}$ – 145 kt – approximately 30 seconds after Brake Release after a roll of about 3500 ft from the start of the roll. The crash aircraft reached V_{LOF} somewhere between 140 – 145 kt in 45 seconds, using about 5400 ft.

The most probable cause of the accident was the failure of the flight crew to use engine de-icing, allied with the failure of the captain to abort the takeoff early, once his attention had been drawn to '. . . anomalous engine instrument readings . . .'. (This statement should, surely, have been qualified. His attention, according to the CVR record, was only called to the opinion – unspecified – of the first officer that something was not right.). Also, due to the ice and snow accretion the aircraft was aerodynamically distorted, with a significantly raised V_S. For the same essential reason – icing – although the engines were fully serviceable they were each producing substantially less thrust than was required (10 750 lb each instead of 14 500 lb) simply because the throttles had only been moved to a position to give 1.70 EPR, while 2.04 was being indicated and was the value required. In other words, the accident was substantially due to incorrect engine instrument reading, yet occurring at the same time on two separate instruments for two different engines. These two factors combined to produce a very significantly reduced acceleration – aerodynamic drag reduced plus reduced power. The aircraft, in fact, used nearly 2000 ft excess to that required in the acceleration to V_1.

Somewhat earlier in this analysis, reference was made to a nose-high attitude and a pronounced sink. The B737 was known to be prone to the first characteristic when its wings were contaminated, and the V_S became raised as a result. The sink may have been due to the high angle of attack, coupled with the fact that the stick-shaker operated at a much higher speed than theoretical V_S, thus indicating that the aircraft was, in fact, at least close to the stall, even though V_S should have been some 20% lower. But the sink could have been caused by the ground effect profile, the aircraft following the consequent air 'cushion' down from the runway to the river, from which it slowly and laboriously climbed, gradually moving away from V_2 as the speed built up. Had the bridge not been there the aircraft might have been able to complete the takeoff safely.

The report once again refers to the need for a takeoff performance indicator but noted that there was large resistance on the part of much of the industry to the introduction of such an instrument. Yet, once again, had such an instrument been fitted it is almost certain that this accident could have been avoided – always assuming that its indications had been heeded, of course. A suitable instrument had been tested by the FAA in 1977/8 (see Chapter 8).

NTSB Report No. AAR-82-8 refers.

Comment on Appendices B and C

The two accidents referred to in the NTSB Reports cited were selected for two reasons. They occurred just over 11 years apart, thus highlighting the lack of response to the NTSB's recommendations, particularly regarding the need for distance to be integrated with speed during the takeoff, *visually*. In both of these accidents the aircraft was not where its pilot thought it was during the takeoff roll, and by a very significantly reduced degree at that. But how can a pilot know how far he has rolled when V_1 is coming up if his sole reference is the ASI? V_1 will be 'bugged', as will V_R and V_2. Why cannot a 'DGI' (Distance Gone Indicator) be included in the instrumentation, and the appropriate distances 'bugged'? The authorities will say that, because of the many variables that are involved, it is difficult to select the distance values that match the speeds. Too much accuracy, it is implied, may result in unnecessarily aborted takeoffs. But the data contained in the *Certificated* Flight Manual is based almost entirely on speed v distance relationships, under varying conditions.

The second reason for comparing these two accidents was the similarity of the prevailing conditions. Both were night takeoffs, in well below freezing temperatures, and with ice and snow present. The pilot in the DC-8 accident had no chance, and cannot be criticised. Who could reasonably expect a degree of runway icing such that it would allow a large aircraft to literally slide the length of the runway with all main wheels locked? In the 737 accident, if only the first officer had specified *why* he thought that things were not right he might have prevented that accident. The moral to this is simple: if something is wrong, in your opinion, say so and say *why*. Don't worry about incurring the wrath of those above you; that can be sorted out later, under calmer, less stress-affected conditions. It is difficult to do this, as the author knows himself, being guilty of an even worse offence – total silence. As a young co-pilot at the time, in the Air Force, he noted well into a takeoff that the Flaps were fully down in the landing position. He decided to stay quiet because a high speed had already been attained, while accelerate:stop was not then 'invented'. It appeared to be safer to continue with the takeoff than to either retract the flaps or to distract the aircraft commander. As there was no engine failure the aircraft became safely airborne and Undercarriage Up was selected. Then, and only then, did the author draw the commander's attention to the flaps. The response was, very contritely, 'That was very naughty of me!', and no reprimand to the author – but there should have been.

Although only two 'distance:speed related' accidents have been discussed it should not be assumed that these were the only two. In that 11 year period in question there had been several more. Conditions varied, but in each case undetected takeoff acceleration degradation, *without engine failure,* played its part. In view of the industry's reluctance to provide a solution to the problem, the only constructive advice that can be offered to pilots is to know the various elements involved in the scheduling of takeoff performance far beyond the basic requirements for the passing of the examination.

Glossary of Terms and Abbreviations

Altitude

Density Altitude	The theoretical density of a standard atmosphere at that altitude.
Pressure Altitude	The altitude shown on an altimeter when the sub-scale is set to 1013.2 mb or 29.92 in. Hg.
True Altitude	The absolute altitude, or as close to this as is possible, using instrumentation fitted to an aircraft.
ISA	International Standard Atmosphere. 1013.2 mb/29.92 in Hg at msl at 15°C, reducing by roughly 1°C per 500 ft in altitude – e.g. ISA at 2000 ft is 11°C, at 6000 ft is 3°C, at 16 000 ft is −17°C and so on.

Speed

ASIR	The Air Speed Indicator Reading in an aircraft.
CAS	Calibrated Air Speed. This is equal to ASIR, corrected for both position and instrument errors. (CAS = TAS at msl at ISA.)
EAS	Equivalent Air Speed. This is equal to ASIR, corrected for position error, instrument error, and compressibility for altitude. (EAS = CAS at msl at ISA.)
IAS	ASIR corrected for instrument error only.
TAS	True Air Speed. Speed relative to the outside air.
V_{EF}	The speed at which an engine fails, or is assumed to fail.
V_1	Takeoff Decision Speed.
V_R	Rotation Speed. The speed when the aircraft taking off assumes a position for flight (lift-off).
V_{MCG}	Minimum Control Speed – ground.
V_{MCA}	Minimum Control Speed – airborne.
V_{MU}	Minimum Unstick Speed CAS.
V_{LOF}	Lift-off Speed.

GLOSSARY

V_2	Takeoff Safety Speed. Not less than $1.2\times$ Stalling Speed for configuration.
V_3	Initial Steady Climb Speed, all-engines operating at Screen Height for V_2 (35 ft).
V_4	Steady Climb Speed, with Undercarriage Up and Flaps at Takeoff.
V_{FC}	Final Climb Speed (Takeoff).
V_{MBE}	Maximum Speed for Brake Energy absorption capability.
V_{FR}	Flap Retraction Safety Speed.
V_{FTO}	Final Takeoff Speed.
V_{AT_1}	Target Threshold Speed – one engine out.
V_{AT_0}	Target Threshold Speed – all engines out.
V_{MT}	Minimum Threshold Speed.
V_{MC_L}	Minimum Control Speed for Landing Approach, all-engines.
V_P	Aquaplaning Speed.
V_S	Stalling Speed for the appropriate configuration.
V_{S_0}	Stalling Speed for Approach Flaps, Undercarriage Up.
V_{S_1}	Stalling Speed for any case under consideration.
$V_{S_{1g}}$	Stalling Speed for a force equalling $1\times$ Gravity.
V_{MS}	Minimum Speed in the Stall.
V_{TD}	Touch down Speed.
V_{TMAX}	Maximum speed at landing threshold.
TTS	Target Threshold Speed.

Weights

MTOW	Maximum Permitted Takeoff Weight, structural.
MLW	Maximum Landing Weight, structural.
MZFW	Maximum Weight of aircraft excluding fuel. This is a Limiting Weight and any increase may only comprise fuel.
RTOW	Regulated Takeoff Weight. The takeoff weight (Maximum) permitted by runway, altitude, temperature, or obstacle clearance.
RLW	The Landing Weight (Maximum) permitted by runway and altitude, or by Approach Climb WAT requirements.
MLW	Maximum Landing Weight.
Maximum auw	Maximum all-up weight (similar to MTOW).

GLOSSARY

OWE	Operating Weight Empty.
APS	Aircraft Prepared for Service Weight.

Temperature

OAT	Outside Air Temperature. The Temperature outside the aircraft in undisturbed air.
ISA	See *Altitude*.
T_{FLEX}	The temperature used when calculating power reduction for Reduced Thrust takeoff.

Runway Distances

TORA	Takeoff Run Available.
EMDA/ASDA	Accelerate-Stop Distance Available.
TODA	Takeoff Distance Available.
LDA	Landing Distance Available.
TORR	Takeoff Run Required.
EMDR/ASDR	Accelerate-Stop Distance Required.
TODR	Takeoff Distance Required.
LDR	Landing Distance Required.

Engine Parameters

EPR	Engine Pressure Ratio $\left(\dfrac{Pt_7}{Pt_2}\right)$.
Pt_2	Inlet Pressure.
Pt_7	Exhaust Pressure.
N_1	Low pressure Compressor rpm.
N_2	High pressure Compressor rpm.
rpm	revolutions per minute.
TBO	Time Between Overhauls.
EGT	Exhaust Gas Temperature.

General

JAR 25	European Joint Airworthiness Requirements (Part 25).
FAR 25	Federal Aviation Regulations (Part 25).
BCARs	British Civil Airworthiness Requirements.
FAA	Federal Aviation Administration.
Australian DCA	Australian Director of Civil Aviation's Requirements.
AIP	Aeronautical Information Publication.
ICAO	International Civil Aviation Organisation.

GLOSSARY

WAT	Weight, Altitude and Temperature.
amsl	above mean sea level.
SG	Specific Gravity.
WED	Water Equivalent Depth.
ISWL	Isolated Single Wheel Load.
LCN	Load Classification Number.
RZ	Reference Zero for Takeoff Flight Path.
psi	pounds per square inch.
NPRM	Notice of Proposed Rule Making (FAA).
AOM	Aerodrome Operating Minima.
C of G	Centre of Gravity.
nm	Nautical mile.
VOR	Very High Frequency Omnidirectional Radio Range.
FL	Flight Level.
ETA	Expected Time of Arrival.
nampkg	nautical air miles per kg.
RVR	Runway Visual Range.
fpm	feet per minute.
G/P	Glide Path.
W/V	Wind Velocity.
G/S	Ground Speed.
IFR	Instrument Flight Rules.
C_{DG}	Coefficient of drag-ground.
C_{DA}	Coefficient of drag-air.
BTG	British Technology Group (UK).
NRDC	National Research Development Corporation (UK).
NTSB	National Transportation Safety Board (USA).
USAF	United States Air Force.
CVR	Cockpit Voice Recorder.
FMS	Flight Management Systems.
FDR	Flight Data Recorder.
DGI	Distance Gone Indicator.
TOPM	Takeoff Performance Monitoring Systems.
BEA	British European Airways.
u/c	undercarriage.

Index

(See also Glossary, pages 135–7)

Aborted takeoff, 99
Acceleration Distance, 55, 56
ACJs, 47
Aerad, 2
Aerodrome Operating Minima (AOM), 77
AIP, 2
Air Navigation (General) Regulations (UK), 15
Alternate aerodrome, 17, 76, 93
Altitude
  Density, 101
  Pressure, 8, 101
amsl, 8
Amsterdam (Schiphol), 8
Anchorage, 122
Approach, 7 *et al.*
Aquaplaning, 47
ASD, 3 *et al.*
ASDA, 3 *et al.*
auw, 14

BAe 146–100, 28 *et al.*
Balanced Field, 4
Baulked Landing, 97, 117
BCARs, 21 *et al.*
Brake Energy Limits, 35, 119, 120, 121

Cabin, Rate of Descent, 83
C_{DA}, 92
C_{DG}, 92
Centre of Gravity (C of G), 75
Certificated Performance, 17 *et al.*
Clearway, 1 *et al.*
Cockpit Voice Recorder (CVR), 128
Contaminated Runway, 50, 51, 52
Cruise, 17

'D' value, 30, 31, 32, 33, 34 *et al.*
DCA (Australia), 21

DC3/Dakota, 10
Decision Height (DH), 95
Decision Point, 2, 6, 11, 12 *et al.*
Decision Speed, 2, 11, 12 *et al.*
Delays, time, 26
Density Altitude, 8, 10
Descent, 17, 83, 84
Destination aerodrome, 17, 93
Discontinues Approach, 95, 96
Displaced Threshold, 4
Distance Gone Indicator, 133
Drag, 25, 29 *et al.*
Drift Down, 78, 79

EAS, 81
EGT, 126
Elevation, 13
EMDA, 3, 24, *et al.*
Emergency Distance Available, 3 *et al.*
Engine instrumentation, 112
En route, 75
EPR, 27, 45 *et al.*

factoring, 12, 23, 38, 87, 88
FAR 25, ix, 3 *et al.*
FAR 121, ix
Federal Aviation Administration (FAA) (USA), 20
Flight Data Recorder (FDR), 122
Flight Level, 16
Flight Manual, 2 *et al.*
Flight Path, 17, 59
Fokker F27, 6, 7, 37, 53, 54, 55, 104
Fokker F28, 37, 54, 55, 104, 105

Gross Flight Path, 60 *et al.*
Gross Performance, 23 *et al.*

ICAO, 20
Indicated Air Speed (IAS), 12 *et al.*

140   INDEX

Innsbruck, 7
International Standard Atmosphere (ISA), 8 *et al.*

Joint Airworthiness Requirements, JAR 25, ix, 3 *et al.*

KLM, 10
Kondor, 11
Kurier, 11

Landing Distance, 2, 17, 83, 117 *et al.*
Landing Distance Available (LDA), 3 *et al.*
Load Classification No. (LCN), 57
Lift, 29
Limitations, absolute, 38

Maximum Continuous Power (MCP), 17
Missed Approach, 17, 85
Mombasa, 92

N_1, 130
N_2, 126
Nairobi, 92
Net Flight Path, 17, 59, 60, 61, 62, 63, 64 *et al.*
Net Performance, 23, 114
National Transportation Safety Board (NTSB) (USA), 122, 127, 128, 130, 132

Obstacle Clearance Requirements, 59
Overspeed techniques, 54

Performance Schedule, 11
Precipitation, 47, 50
Pressure Altitude, 8
Pt_2, 130

Ratio
  $V_1 : V_R$, 12
  $V_1 : V_2$, 12
Reduced Thrust, 44, 45
Reference Touchdown Speed, 94
Reference Zero, 64 *et al.*
Requirements, Performance, 20 *et al.*
Reverse Thrust, 22
Risks, flight, 18
Rolling Start, 44, 45

RTOW, 43 *et al.*
Runway, 1 *et al.*

Safety Speed – takeoff, 3
Sandringham, 11
Screen Height, 3 *et al.*
Segments, Flight Path, 22, 60, 61, 62, 63, 67
Short Field Performance, 115, 116
Slope, 1, 5, 8 *et al.*
Small airliners, 113
Solent, 11
Stabilising Altitude, 78, 79, 80, 81
Standard Deviation, 13
Stopping distance, 55
Stopway, 1, 4 *et al.*
Stratocruiser, 11
Sunderland, 11

Takeoff Distance Available (TODA), 2, 3 *et al.*
Takeoff Flight Path, 43, 59, 60
Takeoff instrumentation, 107, 108, 109, 110, 111, 112
Takeoff Run Available (TORA), 2, 3 *et al.*
Takeoff Safety Speed, 115
Target Threshold Speed (TTS), 92
TBO, 43
Temperature, ambient, 24
Tflex, 45
TOD4, 15
Turn, 68
Type 'A' Chart, 7
Tyre Speed Limit, 24, 56, 57, 119

Unclassified aircraft, 2

V_{AT}, 89
V_{AT_0}, 89
V_{AT_1}, 89
V_{EF}, 26, 60
V_{FR}, 71
V_{LOF}, 2 *et al.*
V_{MBE}, 12, 56, 119, 120, 121
V_{MC}, 22
V_{MC_A}, 16
V_{MC_G}, 16
V_{MC_L}, 91, 92
V_{MS}, 97, 136

V_{MS_1}, 71
V_{MU}, 16
VOR, 76
V_S, 3, 24 *et al.*
V_{S_0}, 92
V_{Tmax}, 89
V_1, 2, 26 *et al.*
V_1 Wet, 27 *et al.*
V_R, 14 *et al.*
V_2, 3, 14
V_3, 41, 136
V_4, 136

Washington DC, 128
WAT, 11, 24, 30 *et al.*
Water Equivalent Depth (WED), 47
Weight
  APS, 102
  OWE, 102
Weights, standard, 102
Wind Shear, 106

York, Avro, 11